# Navigating the Workplace

# Navigating the Workplace

## What School Executives Should Know about Labor Relations

Richard D. Tomko

ROWMAN & LITTLEFIELD
*Lanham • Boulder • New York • London*

Published by Rowman & Littlefield
An imprint of The Rowman & Littlefield Publishing Group, Inc.
4501 Forbes Boulevard, Suite 200, Lanham, Maryland 20706
www.rowman.com

86-90 Paul Street, London EC2A 4NE

Copyright © 2022 by Richard D. Tomko

*All rights reserved.* No part of this book may be reproduced in any form or by any electronic or mechanical means, including information storage and retrieval systems, without written permission from the publisher, except by a reviewer who may quote passages in a review.

British Library Cataloguing in Publication Information Available

**Library of Congress Cataloging-in-Publication Data**

Names: Tomko, Richard D., 1973– author.
Title: Navigating the workplace : what school executives should know about labor relations / Richard D. Tomko.
Description: Lanham, Maryland : Rowman & Littlefield, 2022.
Identifiers: LCCN 2022014898 (print) | LCCN 2022014899 (ebook) |
  ISBN 9781475862546 (cloth) | ISBN 9781475862553 (paperback) | ISBN 9781475862560 (ebook)
Subjects: LCSH: Collective bargaining—Teachers—United States. | Collective labor agreements—Education—United States. | Teachers' unions—United States. | Teacher-administrator relationships—United States. | Educational leadership—United States.
Classification: LCC LB2844.59.U6 T66 2022 (print) | LCC LB2844.59.U6 (ebook) | DDC 331.88/1137110973—dc23/eng/20220510
LC record available at https://lccn.loc.gov/2022014898
LC ebook record available at https://lccn.loc.gov/2022014899

This book is dedicated to my wife of twenty-two years and my best friend, Jaimie. You have been nothing but a true inspiration and my greatest "cheerleader" since the first day we met each other back in high school. The knowledge that I gained throughout my administrative career and, in turn, my ability to continue to create true "playbooks" like this one to assist the future leaders of tomorrow is only possible because of your eagerness to listen to the daily trials and tribulations of my job while acting as my voice of reason when times seemed like they were never going to get any easier.

Your resilience, fortitude, and ability to stand by me while giving up many of your own dreams and goals is a debt to you that I will never be able to repay. You continue to support me and our children to ensure that we always do what is right, just, and necessary to help make this world a better place. For that and much more, I continue to fall in love with you over and over again with each new day, and I am in awe of you as a provider, parent, a mom—and just an all-around incredible person.

I appreciate you.

I will hold your heart, forever.

—RT

*Memento vivere*

La·bor

*Noun*
1. work, especially hard physical work.

*Verb*
1. work hard; make great effort.
2. have difficulty in doing something despite working hard.

We are what we repeatedly do. Excellence then, is not an act, but a habit.

—Aristotle

# Contents

| | |
|---|---|
| Preface | xiii |
| Introduction | 1 |
| Chapter 1: Education, Personnel, and the Labor Movement | 5 |
| Chapter 2: Organizational Hierarchy | 11 |
| Chapter 3: History of Unions and Organized Labor | 17 |
| Chapter 4: Politics in the Workplace | 25 |
| Chapter 5: The Importance of the Labor-Management Relationship | 29 |
| Chapter 6: Labor Laws | 37 |
| Chapter 7: Labor Defined among Industries | 41 |
| Chapter 8: Leading Together | 49 |
| Chapter 9: Power | 53 |
| Chapter 10: Negotiating to Win | 59 |
| Chapter 11: Contracts, Agreements, "Handshakes," and Past Practice | 63 |
| Chapter 12: It's Not What You're Selling, It's How You're Selling It | 69 |
| Chapter 13: When to "Go to the Mattresses" | 73 |
| Chapter 14: Communication Is Key | 77 |
| Chapter 15: Trust | 81 |
| Chapter 16: Strong Leadership on Both Sides | 85 |
| Chapter 17: The Willingness to Make Concessions | 89 |
| Chapter 18: The Art of Negotiation | 93 |

| | |
|---|---:|
| Chapter 19: Response to Actions | 97 |
| Chapter 20: Anti-union Animus | 103 |
| Chapter 21: Pyrrhic Victories and Strategies of Labor Unions | 107 |
| Chapter 22: Avoiding Work Actions | 111 |
| Chapter 23: To Be or Not to Be: When Something Is or Isn't the Appropriate Decision | 117 |
| Chapter 24: The Goldilocks Approach: Not Too Hot, and Not Too Cold | 123 |
| Chapter 25: Impact of Important Labor Court Cases, Legal Considerations, and Precedents | 133 |
| About the Author | 143 |

# Preface

I didn't get to be part of a football team until I entered high school during my freshman year. I was larger than most thirteen-year-old boys, and the eighth grade "hobby" for my friends and I the entire year prior was lifting weights—which didn't hurt matters. I remember the first few days of practice and having "skull" sessions after to learn the offensive playbook. These sessions were where my coaches would "teach" us the plays, blocking schemes, and skill routes by writing them on the chalkboard as the X's and O's became personified, and they signified what I would be using to win games and outsmart my opponents week after week over the rest of my career.

When I played college ball and the game became extremely competitive, the playbook grew much more complex with more options for each position player to utilize at any given moment—within every possible scenario—in order to dominate an opposing player and assist me in executing my job as effectively as possible. Complexities aside, I came to understand that each play was originally designed to score a touchdown if each of the eleven players on the offense executed their particular part of the play correctly. Although that always sounded like such a simple concept, one thing kept it from being so simple—there were eleven other players from the other team looking to do the same exact thing.

Moving on past college and coaching for many years, I found myself in one spot as an offensive coordinator who designed plays and worked alongside some very incredible athletes and coaches. It was here that I truly understood that as each play was designed to score every single time, there were still several plays that were run to "set up" other plays. In fact, most plays that are run in a series sequence are intended to force defenders to react in anticipation of making a tackle, etc., and a defender will utilize muscle memory to make the same reaction should the same sequence be executed again. Now, insert the fake. Thus, if executed properly, the first play is meant to set up the next play which is meant to produce a score.

Now, I am definitely not that type of person who goes around using clichés to explain the role that sports take in developing explanations for living one's life (we all know one or two of those people). But metaphorically speaking, a sports play that leads one advantage into the next easily relates to the strategy, procedures, and processes of the steps one may use in effectively navigating the workplace, politics, and conflicts with personnel and union leadership.

As I elevated through leadership positions in different organizations and districts throughout the years, I continued to reference my training and skills from my coaching days to understand how the same play concepts were closely related to relationships with my employees as individuals and with labor leadership (unions/associations). It soon became obvious that certain strategies and tactics that I would employ in specific situations would not only work to end conflicts and negotiate terms, but also establish a pattern of progressive, successful conquests in consideration of future needs of my teams, other stakeholder groups, and constituents.

In fact, designing "plays" to help navigate the concerns and needs of my teams and individuals, who I worked alongside each and every day, allowed me to concentrate on long-term goals while managing short-term expectations. Simply stated, not every decision has to be made to reach the end goal but every decision must be made with that end goal in mind.

An educational executive's playbook in consideration of her relationship with her workforce will expand with each year she advances her career in leadership roles. Some plays will work, and some plays just won't. She will realize quickly which plays work well in certain circumstances and which are her "go to" plays when she really needs a victory. Learning the playbook will allow her to realize that even if she is perceived to have taken a loss at some point it may still be seen as a win in the long run.

Of course, these plays aren't X's and O's. These plays include many different variables that can completely change the way you execute them based on time; location; budget; and many other considerations that an executive may face on any given day. Just like the coach who may choose a different route or different personnel in the rain versus a sunny day, the educational leader must understand what his expected outcome is and who on his team is the most able individual to make it work.

Also, these X's and O's represent individuals—actual people—who wake up each and every day to help the executive meet his mission and help effectuate change and grow progress in a school, district, or organization. His leadership is defined by how he relates to these individuals and what "plays" he uses daily to help them accomplish their goals and meet the threshold of success that they have established for themselves.

Every executive needs a diversified playbook, a great "coaching" staff, and loyal "players" in order to win games and then ultimately, the championship.

Running a company, nonprofit organization, school district, restaurant, or law firm includes understanding your personnel and how to help facilitate their becoming the best they can at what it is that they do.

It's important to remember that coaches never win games—no . . . championships—alone. It takes the entire organization working together towards one ultimate goal in order to be that successful. Those coaches (executives) who work towards perfecting those skills will be revered by individuals from all walks of life, respected by those who work closely with them "in the trenches," and will be studied for their leadership for generations to come.

## HOW TO USE THIS TEXT

The chapters in this text are designed to provide administrators and leaders with background and strategy to help assist them in designing their own "play" calls when dealing with employees, unions, and labor leadership. It is important to note that each individual school system, district, higher education institution, or organization contains its own complex set of rules, policies, and intricacies that must be examined and considered alongside the suggestions throughout this text.

Further, the political landscape is not the same in any two organizations; therefore, a strict and safe balance must be obtained and utilized by the leader at all times. Most important, always discuss decisions and changes with your attorney and/or association by seeking their advice with matters that concern labor laws and personnel. Each state differs in this area, and it is very important that a leader communicates personnel actions with her (or her board/organization) attorney prior to (not after) making a decision.

Each chapter herein contains "Coaches Corner" and "You Make the Call" case study sections to help review the educational leadership message that was set forth in the pages of the chapter and provide a real-life inbox scenario for leaders and aspiring school executives who can discuss different play calls to utilize in specific circumstances. Sharing these discussions among students and leadership teams allows for growth and a sharing of ideas among individuals in the field.

# Introduction

Dispirited, unmotivated, and unappreciated workers cannot compete in a highly competitive world.[1]

Period.

The archaic theories of leadership and managers who always ruled with a tyrannical iron fist and enhanced employee production through fear are long gone as today's executives must navigate a highly advanced workforce who is more educated, technically savvy, and permeated by the need for belonging to ensure a greater good for centuries to come.

Understandably, by design the definition of a "boss" is clear to all of us at a very young age. As young, developing children we usually are first made aware of the importance of this term when our mother or father describes a work event at home which helps to mold our imagery and understanding. "Ah, the boss was upset today at our numbers, honey" or "I have to stay late tomorrow and get these reports to my boss before I leave."

To be fair, not all first impressions must be flawed. Maybe the first recall from memory brings you back to a family holiday office party where mom, dad, and your older sister were receiving hugs from an older gentleman who was handing out presents in a tie and Santa hat, with everyone smiling and laughing at his jokes.

Is that out of fear?

Could be.

Or maybe—just maybe—the definition from those early memories includes an individual who understands that he is only as successful as his least productive worker.

As an entrepreneur, one can dream of success in building her empire from an idea for a service or a product that will change the world. A school superintendent leads his district to earning high-achieving status on standardized test scores and college acceptances. The proprietor of a restaurant smiles proudly as he watches a family leave his establishment impressed by their experience, providing him with a reminder of his receiving the county award for "Best

Service" three years in a row. The foreman on a construction site watches intently as his crew finishes placing the final steel beam to signify the start of the next phase of the New City Hospital project that will serve the citizens and create jobs for the metropolitan area.

Although each of these scenarios define successful leadership outside very separate industries or careers, they each have one rather simple phenomenon in common—positive labor relations. Success can only be attained when executive management understands, respects, and can meet the needs of its labor force over many different areas. To be very clear, this is the absolute definition of a successful workplace.

Widget production cannot be quick and safe, test scores halted from exponential increases, and patrons not seen returning to businesses if the relationship between labor units, individuals, and management is not both amicable and respected. This is not to mean that leaders need to be "weak," or "give in" to the demands of the employees and their representative outfits or face a stoppage or retaliation. Rather, one can argue that a leader who keeps his team and organization "happy" or at least on pleasant terms in consideration of contractual obligations and workplace policies and procedures will maintain the greatest output of production.

As a young school administrator, I can recall one of my first times reprimanding a seasoned employee. Nervous, I entered the meeting determined to ensure that this employee would be "taught a lesson." I came to the meeting overly prepared, practically memorizing the personnel file of the veteran individual sitting across from me. His union representative, older and disheveled, was a few minutes late, and I reviewed the ground rules for the fact-finding meeting.

I began my review of the reprimand, tending to be direct and surgical with my diction while utilizing the methods of a jurist who was attempting to outline a legal argument. "I know, I know," the employee responded. "And I get it . . . you're the boss. Hey, I didn't want this to happen either." At that moment, I had reached an epiphany at such an early point in my administrative career. Simply put—not every mistake is egregious.

The absence of controversy is an ultimate goal for workers and managers alike. No one wants or expects any adverse dealings at the workplace on a daily basis. In fact, one can argue that an uncomplicated workday in consideration of relationships and protocols equals true success. Hence, there is a strong correlation between the success of any leader/manager and the relationship she has with her employees and staff.

In all, an educational leader as an executive must utilize all of her interpersonal skills, political sense, and leadership qualities to help direct the mission of her organization to growing success beyond those competitors in her industry or field. Competition in nearly every aspect of our world is real—and nothing sits closer to the truth than when we discuss how competition affects each individual's professional goals and future.

Whether it is in the for-profit or nonprofit arenas, a local government post, a national research institute, university, school district, or the corner market store in a tiny suburb of Connecticut, one thing is certain: the relationship between management and labor must always come together and work towards the same purpose in order for everyone involved to benefit.

## NOTE

1. Francis Hesselbein, *Hesselbein on Leadership* (San Francisco: Jossey-Bass, 2002).

*Chapter 1*

# Education, Personnel, and the Labor Movement

To an outsider, the world that exists in consideration of educating an individual from preschool to postsecondary institutions of learning may seem to contain a daily cavalcade of individuals with books, curricula, and programs to shape the career paths of individual adolescent and adult "students" who learn to advance their knowledge in a particular discipline or area of interest. In fact, it has been argued that teachers, professors, administrators, and the like are solely responsible for the professional trajectory of an individual over the course of their academic career.

The plain truth of the matter is that the field of education contains a much more meandering highway of intricate systems that each add a supportive cog to a wheel representing a significant but somewhat "hidden" industry of global proportions. The business of education is such that teachers, administrators, and other stakeholder organizations work together to produce the most important widget[1] of any historic industry, business, or organization.

That widget is people. And with the production of an individual's future comes many outside needs, influencers, and "wants" to help ensure that the industry of education remains lucrative to vendors, consultants, and companies where during the 2017–2018 school year, total expenditures for public elementary and secondary schools in the United States reached $762 billion, or $14,891 per enrolled student.[2]

Regardless of the budget a particular city or local school district creates or the color of the basketball jerseys it decides on for the girls' basketball team, the simple fact will always remain that nothing—and I mean nothing—in education and other related fields escalates success more in any work environment than positive and productive personnel. The labor force that a leader, administrator, or manager creates must not only be competent, academic, and ethical but also be able to operate around personal issues and other relevant needs to ensure a productive staff will lead to the most positive of outcomes.

Effectively navigating the workplace, politics, and conflicts with personnel and union leadership is not something that must become second nature to leaders and administrators in the field of education. As with any other company, corporation, nonprofit, or government organization, the leader of a district, department, university, or school continuously makes daily decisions that affect the outcome, production, and needs of his constituents.

Individuals tend not to relate education to other industries or businesses in the global arena; however, on the contrary, the success of an educational institution leads to greater student preparation for careers; higher market value for homes and real estate; and the enhancement of "quality of life" for individuals relatively close to the institution.

Further, products and vendors in consideration of materials, technology, and other operational and facility needs make a major contribution to crossover industries who bid public projects and invest in private educational ventures. Many budgets for school systems and universities total more than the city, town, or even the county in which they are located.

Now add the labor aspect of the field into the mix and a complete picture comes to the forefront of how education and the business-world are not too far off from one another, where many of the tenets of process and production seem to overlap. Again, the widgets aren't the same, but how to facilitate the production of them is very close.

More evident that labor plays a major role is the fact that most educational institutions are either the largest or second-largest individual employer in a particular city, town, or area, where it is projected that there will be more than 3.2 million full-time teachers in the U.S. in the fall of 2022.[3] Such a large labor force is indicative of the need for distinct human resources services and other important professional development measures as well as appropriate managerial oversight within each individual organization.

Thus, as the needs of the workplace expand in the field of education, just like every other industry, individual labor leaders emerge as well as organized labor unions where today nearly 70 percent of all teachers in the United States are members.[4]

As far back as 1857, educators first united to increase teacher salaries, enhance working conditions, strengthen child labor laws, and educate emancipated slaves. That year, forty-three educators came together in Philadelphia, Pennsylvania to create the National Education Association (NEA). Almost 20 years later in 1916 Chicago, founders established the AFL-backed American Federation of Teachers (AFT) in what is known as the first organized labor movement for education in America. In 2019, the NEA and the AFT boasted a membership of nearly 2.3 million and 1.7 million active and retired educators, respectively.[5]

As organized labor movements grew in other industries throughout the United States to assist workers in their fight for fair wages, better working conditions, and a chance to bargain the operations and obligations of the workplace, educators realized that union association would benefit their career paths in appreciation of salary, benefits, evolving tenure laws, and academic freedom.

Hence, the call for action in response to the ever-changing societal norms and obligations of working-class citizens in white-collar industries like the field of education helped to grow the need for labor unions to organize local chapters in cities and towns throughout the country.

With the growth of organized labor in schools, an added level of oversight and "checks and balances" was infused into the daily routines of the workday, increasing the oversight of leadership and administrative teams to include the leadership of labor associations and unions.

As educational leadership includes multiple facets of managerial strategy, academic prowess, effective supervision, and the creation and implementation of policy that affect all employees and members of the organization, the ability for the chief executive to work in tandem with labor leaders to ensure workplace readiness and productivity creates an extra influential "layer" that school personnel have to insulate them from some of the outliers that work against the mission of the industry in consideration of both local and national standards.

Figure 1.1 shows the 4 levels of influence of educational personnel with regard to both outside and internal systems. As an industry employee establishes a strict work ethic and means by which she values her organization, the same holds true for faculty, administration, and staff members in the field of education.

As depicted, Level 1 includes those stated values closest to the individual's experiences and upbringing that create the first layer of influencers to help the employee make decisions and respond to interactions in consideration of his own needs and utility. Several of these influencers stem from familial ties, cultural norms, and the individual's own moral compass.

Level 2 influencers dictate the major components of the job to the employee, and they indicate the need to conform to a system that is put in place by constituent groups to create a standard for the educational field and what should be valued by the individual in consideration of successful job performance. These influencers provide important direction, strategies, and tools to systematic personnel to ensure successful job performance through the provision of information, development, and capital in order to meet agency demands.

Level 3 insulates each member further by creating boundaries and oversight to help direct personnel through the appropriate channels to meet the

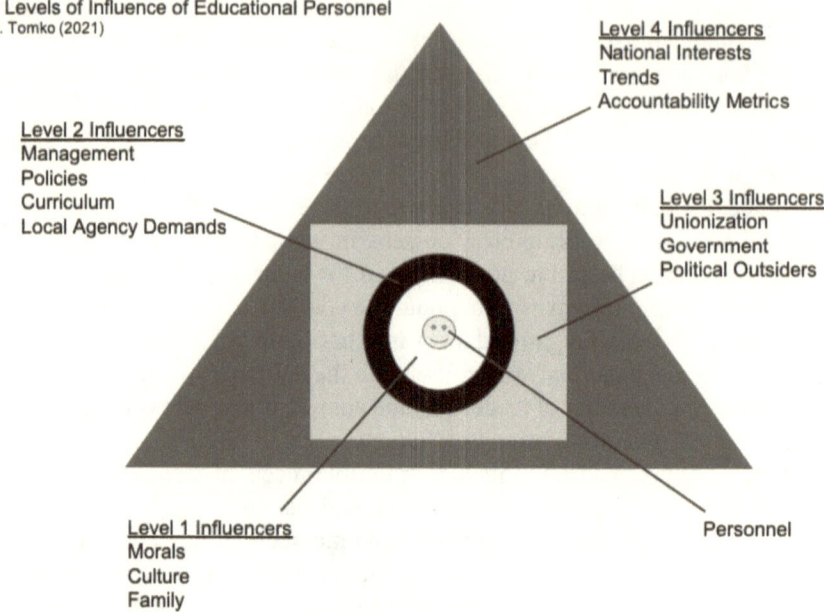

Figure 1.1. 4 Levels.

standards derived from the previous level. Here, government and other outside political factors weigh in on certification needs, mandates, and changes to the laws and statutes created to provide a broad sense of the academic needs of citizens and the policies set forth to govern the processing of those needs.

It is also at this level that unionization adds to the political landscape, working parallel to the organization's leadership team while further insulating personnel from outside influencers that may bring harm to the system and the individual.

Adding to the overall scrutiny in a broad sense are the Level 4 influencers that cast a wide net over the entire system on the basis of national interests, suitable trends, and other metrics (like test scores) to hold all individuals accountable and provide comparison from one organization to the next. Here at Level 4, one begins to find where a union holds its interests as it continues to insulate the employee from outside influencers that may not benefit the goals of the organization.

In a sense, it is imperative that the leader understands and acknowledges how the different levels of outside influencers push, pull, and pressure the organization as a whole and each of the individual members of the educational labor force. Understanding where labor leadership treads within such a system will strengthen the executive's ability to effectively navigate her workplace, the politics that permeate throughout the system, and any conflicts that may arise with personnel.

In all, school executives who work alongside their labor force and labor associations must lead not much differently than any other executive in other businesses and organizations that operate to meet specified goals and objectives. Throughout this text, the reader will come to understand how many of the strategies, "plays," and best practices are interchangeable across industry standards. In order to deal with labor in any industry, the executive must be a strong proponent of expanding human capital and respecting the needs of her labor force.

The school executive must also direct her efforts at relieving her plight of management and labor associations, especially with labor/union leaders, which must always be adversarial in nature. Regardless, one thing holds steadfast in consideration of how the widgets are produced—if the workers in the trenches aren't successful in production, the executive won't be successful in the organization.

## COACHES CORNER

Educational leaders must learn to work day-in and day-out with personnel and labor leadership. Whether it be a union in a K–12 district, adjunct faculty at a local college, or a respected "liaison" for a small group of assistants, the benefits of working to ensure successful personnel and labor relationships can be great if the administrator works to meet the needs of his people.

In the field of education, leaders on both sides sometimes allow their pride to get in the way of making appropriate decisions that will have both positive and negative effects on all stakeholder groups. The influence they share can define the outcome of a goal or even halt progress that is stopped by team members or employees who don't feel they are being listened to.

Educational leaders, regardless of their position, connection to students, or the level of industry they are in, must concentrate on navigating the workplace in an appropriate manner to ensure they gain the most benefit from their relationship with labor and personnel.

## YOU MAKE THE CALL: CASE SCENARIO

The union president from your district, John Solare, asks to see you about a situation that has been relayed to him from one of the elementary schools. During your meeting, he explains that several employees are upset because they feel that their evaluations completed by the building supervisor were unfair in consideration of their community engagement throughout the school system.

After John told you the staff members who were making the formal complaint, you were surprised that two of them were not given a fair rating in the area of professional responsibilities and district engagement. You do recall that the supervisor did discuss the performance of these staff members during your last administrative meeting, but he never mentioned any concerns.

John explained that he was ready to file an unfair labor practice claim against the administration, stating that this was retaliation on those individual staff members because the supervisor had not been invited to their winter celebration at the local bar and grill that they had planned for the staff. John went on further, telling you he had "heard" that the supervisor was complaining to other staff members that he "wasn't invited on purpose," and "yeah, we'll see who gets the last laugh!"

What plays do you call?
How do you separate the different situations that are occurring here? How would you prioritize your actions?
What matters (if any) would you investigate? If you choose to investigate, what are some of the policy protocols that you must follow while investigating these matters?
How do you maintain and/or strengthen your relationship with John while handling this situation?

## NOTES

1. An unnamed or hypothetical article that can be manufactured (usually a business term).

2. U.S. Department of Education, National Center for Education Statistics. (2021). *The Condition of Education 2021* (NCES 2021-144), Public School Expenditures.

3. U.S. Department of Education, National Center for Education Statistics, Statistics of Public Elementary and Secondary Day Schools, 1955–56 through 1980–81; Statistics of Nonpublic Elementary and Secondary Schools, 1955 through 1980; 1983–84, 1985–86, and 1987–88 Private.

4. U.S. Department of Education, National Center for Education Statistics, National Teacher and Principal Survey (NTPS), "Public School Teacher Data File," 2017–18.

5. Madeline Will, "Nation's Largest Teachers' Union Sees Slight Upswing in Membership," *Education Week*, June 14, 2019; Madeline Will, "Teachers' Unions Expected Big Membership Losses. Here's Why Those Haven't Panned Out," *Education Week*, June 27, 2019.

*Chapter 2*

# Organizational Hierarchy

The structure and organizational hierarchy of any organization is an important tool in assuring that appropriate reporting lines are understood and followed in consideration of chain of command, policy creation, and promotional pathways. Comprehending the different types of structures and why each is effective is instrumental in navigating the organizational "highway" of any office or labor force.

This holds true on both the management and the labor "side." There is a direct order and protocols to reporting issues that concern any organization and how that organization would choose to operate in consideration of the issue at hand. The most practical practice in solving any conflict or disagreement is to direct the individual with the complaint or concern to the immediate-level supervisor or manager that is involved in the situation. Simply stated, this is the individual with whom the problem has occurred, and there should at least be an opportunity for the situation to come to a resolution at this level.

The ability to resolve any conflict at the source itself is not only great from a conflict resolution standpoint, but it also strengthens the relationship between the employees involved, and it also builds confidence within the morale of the organization. Working with individuals includes a partnership not unlike any other partnership—personal and business—in our daily lives. There will be good times and bad times, disagreements and windfalls, as well as the day when someone is just in a "bad" mood. As most of us are programmed with a competitive spirit to persevere and win any type of conflict, compromising at times, or understanding when you are in the wrong as an individual, moves the mission a very long way.

The ability to work through issues at the level of leadership and labor force where they actually occurred is the easiest and quickest way to strengthen the working relationship of the organization and foster a stronger work ethic in the team. This holds true since both sides feel that they are being heard and their concerns are recognized with regard to importance and a sense of true urgency to make things work.

Without this first-level compromise, problems can escalate to upper levels of the organizational hierarchy, and this leads to others dealing with issues, placing their own perspective on why the issue had occurred in the first place, but most importantly, it negates any push for understanding and relationship building with regard to conflict resolution that the initial parties have.

As the urgency then focuses on keeping the conflict and its resolution to "first"-level discussions, there are several methods, strategies, and techniques that can be utilized to help mediate the situation into a fully resolved outcome.

## USE A HUMBLE BUT STERN TONE WHEN MEDIATING

This may sound contradictory, but it is truly an important step in the mediation process when considering one's role as an organizational leader and his ability to control any type of conflict resolution with the labor force. As an executive in the educational organization, he is still the driving force behind the mission that the system needs to meet on a daily basis.

To enhance production and manufacture outstanding "widgets," the administrator needs to continue to acknowledge that the entire labor force must be trained, competent, and feel respected. This leads to a higher level of morale within the organization, school, or district as well as providing the administrator or leader with a strong foundation on which to build greater production levels and a sense of pride in performance within the organizational structure. No individual or team produces when it is unhappy.

Therefore, when attempting to mediate the original concern, a manager/administrator must ensure that her body language, demeanor, diction, and engagement are humble, and she respects what the employee is feeling. On the surface, she may not agree with the needs or feelings of said employee; however, a compromise or conclusion will never occur at the initial level of the organizational hierarchy if she is not open to seeing the issue from the labor perspective.

A stern tone must also be representative of the discussions that are taking place to ensure that the employee unit has an understanding that you are still leading the charge and facilitating the discussion. This is where a leader finds himself in a predicament, at times, being unable to balance both of these important and emotional descriptors of the leadership role.

To come across as caring and concerned while still pressing one's point to concert managerial "tactics" is truly seen as an art form. There is not much difference between this and the teachable moment that a parent has with her child, listening and advising in an understanding tone so as to ensure the lesson remains cemented in the child's memory. Success is realized when the parent exudes strong and meaningful discipline to solidify her role as a parental unit.

## HAVE FACTS AND EVIDENCE

The easiest and most appropriate way to prove a position or convince someone to move closer to a cause is to provide a factual basis that includes evidentiary artifacts relative to the decisions that were made. There is very little progress to be made in winning any argument if said argument cannot be "backed" by any true reason or process as to why the current situation is occurring.

Trying to work out an issue with members of a team, union leaders, and association representatives should include references to past practices, contract and case law, and protocols that other companies, departments, or organizations follow surrounding similar circumstances.

In fact, it is extremely important to realize that the labor side will most definitely come prepared to mediate with facts and evidence in hand. It is best to hypothesize what that evidence may be in order to prepare well in advance for the mediation session.

One necessary strategy is to utilize data points that are relatively similar to the current physical configuration and culture of the organization in question. For example, when mediating a dress code policy requirement, smaller district offices may look towards policies differently than larger office structures. Rather, it would benefit the leader to find current policies and protocols from successful companies of like size, structure, and makeup.

## PREVIOUSLY PREPARE THE COMPROMISE—
## THE "GIVE AND TAKE"

Prior to any follow-up meeting regarding the issues faced, managers and leadership must have a plan in place that directly relates to a compromise that can be introduced and agreed to in order to keep the decision at the current level of the hierarchy. Again, no one wants to have an issue or disagreement be settled or adjusted by individuals on the team other than those directly related to the issue.

However, in order to truly compromise, a leader/manager must be willing to negotiate and give ground on what the labor team/employees feel is most important to their situation at hand. This should never be considered as "giving in" to employees; rather, an affordable compromise allows the morale of the unit to advance while giving onus to both sides, understanding that the give-and-take method permits each to work through the issues.

In preparing prior to the meeting or conversation related to such a compromise, a leader must lay out a road map of sorts in order to identify the future pros, cons, and complications of the compromise that will be offered. Although it is important to ensure that the labor/employees team gains some benefit in order to reach the compromise, it cannot be excessive due to the fact that such a compromise would negate any benefit of management and the organization as a whole.

Many of these compromises deal with policies and monetary agreements in consideration of personnel. A negotiated contract by definition includes compromised values that both sides agree to that may see gains and losses to accommodate new contractual components that are requested from the workforce.

## COACHES CORNER

In education, following the chain of command is an extremely important process that must be consistently followed throughout the organization. Most educational systems approve specific policies that outline which individuals report to specific administrators and describe the steps for individuals to use when contacting the administrative/supervisory team and following the appropriate chain.

It is imperative that the chief executive respects the protocols and remains consistent in allowing her leadership team to deal with as many issues as possible prior to her getting involved in a decision. First, this provides a safe barrier to ensure she is not micromanaging the organization, and second, she is holding others accountable for doing their jobs.

Much too often, executives get involved in the minutiae of the overall operations of the organization when they already have an organizational structure and hierarchy intact that was created and organized to ensure operational stability. By moving away from the organization infrastructure that was created by strategic design, the leader "blurs" reporting lines used by his labor force and fractures his administrative teams by removing important personnel from making informed decisions.

In educational settings, the hierarchy is in place to ensure that the chain of command provides the most informed decisions to any constituent based upon the input of the individuals directly related to the situation in question. Arguably, it is these individuals who would be best equipped to offer a compromise and ensure that all sides are afforded the greatest opportunity to meet their own needs.

In a K–12 setting, matters would be directed first to an immediate supervisor, then principal, and finally the chief education officer (superintendent/CSA) if the issue still hadn't been resolved. In institutions of higher education, department chairs would handle early issues with professors and students, followed by the dean of the school, provost, vice president, and then president.

At each hierarchical level, organizations with union influence would usually provide members with representation to help discuss the issue at hand. The executive must choose his plays wisely and look at the entire situation prior to excluding a compromise that may pass the issue to the next level. Regardless of need, the chain should never be breached, and the good executive or educational leader ensures that an individual doesn't have the ability to usurp one level of authority to speak with another.

## YOU MAKE THE CALL: CASE SCENARIO

Henry Rubin is a worker in your company for the past fifteen years. Working as a member of your leadership team, Henry asks to speak with you to discuss an issue he is having with a fellow employee. Henry stated that he has never had an issue with anyone before, and he isn't sure "what to do." He figured that since you were the executive officer and once claimed that your door was "always open" when you first arrived seven years ago, that he would just ask you directly.

What plays would you call?
What are your next steps in dealing with the issue at hand?
How do you "follow up" with Henry's needs?

*Chapter 3*

# History of Unions and Organized Labor

Knowing the history of how the American workforce formulated organized labor associations is extremely important in establishing a foundation for any executive who will ultimately need to work alongside union leadership. An historical view allows any leader of a company or organization to understand the deep roots of the movement itself and where the tenets and ideology stem from when considering the mission of labor and the workforce as a whole. This especially holds true for educational leaders and education as an industry.

The school executive who studies the value of the driving force behind his workers will inevitably ensure a productive environment exists in consideration of the day-to-day operations of his organization or institution. A true historical record of the labor movement and rationale behind organizing throughout industries is an extremely large account of incidents, data, and prominent legendary leaders and figureheads who helped shape the current labor movement landscape.

Organized unions and their national labor federations (such as AFL-CIO) have evolved against a backdrop of ever-changing values and priorities with periodic federal government intervention. Volumes of archives have been collected and cited to ensure the established path towards progress is maintained and vetted for accuracy and to provide a true educational resource for leaders across the globe.

Although the purpose of this text is to assist and mentor educational leaders and school administrators in navigating operations in consideration of their workforce, many industries include organized associations that an executive may encounter during her career path. Hence, this chapter provides an attenuated review of some of the major components of the movement in the United States from the early twentieth century to present day.

Labor unions fight for equality, fair wages, and better working conditions. The American working class has always been more ethnically and racially diverse than the middle and upper classes and forms the backbone of industrial labor in the United States.[1] The labor movement grew out of the need to protect the interests of these workers in consideration of better wages, reasonable hours, and safer working conditions. The movement also led efforts to stop child labor, give health benefits to employees, and provide assistance to workers who were injured or retired.[2]

The formation of organized unions spanned the early stages of our formed democracy. Even prior to the signing of the Declaration of Independence, artisans in handicrafts and domestic industry joined together in solidarity to provide members with financial assistance in the event they became ill, incurred debt, or passed away due to their condition.[3] These early alliances had few of the characteristics of present-day unions; however, the associations did have the ability to unite workers with similar skills in order to consider problems of mutual concern and to find solutions for their issues.[4]

With the large-scale influx of transatlantic and rural to urban migration occurring, a larger population of laborers allowed for an increase in labor-intensive enterprises. This increased competition to an unprecedented level, and it limited opportunities that workers had been realizing on their own for some time.[5]

By the early 1800s, journeymen without independent means of production had outnumbered master workers in major cities like New York and Philadelphia,[6] and the need for greater alliances between workers within a similar industry was imminent.

Moving forward to the mid-nineteenth century, industry was booming, and labor was in great demand as prices for products continued soaring upward. The workforce continued focusing its attention on establishing rules around skilled apprenticeship; minimum wage for earners across industries; dues; hiring procedures; and the exclusion of persons not working in the industry.

Enhancements in technology helped to advance innovation and expand markets for industries creating a greater degree of labor organization in larger cities. This prompted the founding of several national unions (the Printers' Union; Stonecutters; Hat Finishers; Molders; Machinists; Locomotive Engineers) which helped to mark the mid-1800s as a time with numerous strikes involving nearly every known craft industry in numerous major cities across the United States. This became the formal push for collective bargaining between unions and management in many leading trades and industries.[7]

As the American dream continued to increasingly grow over time, a steady flow of skilled workers from overseas continued to migrate to industrial America. Skilled American laborers earned higher wages than workers from other countries (e.g., Great Britain), but American laborers worked longer hours, in conditions with greater chances for injuries, and had fewer social services.[8] American industry had the highest rate of accidents in the world,[9] and the only industrial power to have no workman's compensation program in place to support injured workers.[10]

The increased need for more protections leads to the call for more formalized representation and greater alliances among all individuals within a particular industry. In the latter part of the nineteenth century, Samuel Gompers began the Federation of Organized Trades and Labor Unions, which acted to form a partnership of different unions themselves as entities and not individual workers. Gompers's original goal was to persuade the formation of trade unions to help obtain legislation for all contract workers.

The quintessential "organized strike" by labor unions also stemmed from greater organization and became a "routine" event by the late 1800s. There were on record thirty-seven thousand strikes between 1881 and 1905[11] with a majority performed in the building trades and coal mines. The demands of workers included control over working conditions, setting wages, and hiring/firing procedures.

Most of those actions were short in duration, and interestingly enough, during the Great Depression "striking" became more violent but was much less successful since companies were already losing money. Job actions are usually most successful during a period of company or national prosperity when the company or organization would be losing profits and have incentive to negotiate and to settle quickly.[12]

With the global impact and crisis of two world wars in the early part of the twentieth century, organized labor continued to grow productivity in all areas of industry. Women also became a larger part of the movement as their crossover to jobs in industries that were usually male-dominated became more prominent.

At the turn of the century, the Women's Trade Union League was formed (1903) and was the first labor organization charged with helping working women. The union's goal was to support the AFL, encourage more females to join, and provide financial assistance, moral support, and training in workplace readiness skills and social "refinement" for blue-collar women. The organization also lobbied for minimum wages and greater restrictions on child labor while working to pass legislation for wage workers and greater safety regulations.[13]

During World War I, women had been recruited to work jobs that had once been traditionally filled by men who were now overseas or in jobs that had otherwise been solely created to assist the government with manufacturing supplies or providing services directly related to the needs of the war. For example, the immense labor demand for weapons resulted in munitions factories collectively becoming the largest employer of American women by the early part of the twentieth century.

Initial resistance to hiring women for jobs traditionally held by men quickly subsided as the war made the need for labor so urgent that women were hired in extremely large numbers. Governmental recruitment drives urged women to actively take positions in war-related industries.

Thus, women not only began working in heavy industry, but took employment in previously male-dominated industries such as railway guards, ticket collectors, bus conductors, postal workers, police officers, firefighters, and clerks.[14] The Department of Labor also created a Women in Industry group which helped develop standards for women working in war-related industries.[15]

Although every type of movement is initially enveloped within an internal political atmosphere, unions entered national politics in the early twentieth century when they became important allies of the Democratic Party. Labor unions became a central element of the New Deal coalition that dominated national politics from the 1930s into the mid-1960s,[16] and even in recent decades, an enduring alliance was formed between labor unions and the Democrats as the Republican Party has grown hostile to labor associations largely due to philosophical differences in consideration of collective bargaining rights.[17]

In the early 1950s, the AFL and CIO merged and a third of the labor force in the United States was unionized.[18] A rapidly increasing flow of imports in the 1970s (automobiles, steel, electronics, clothing) from Europe and Asia[19] caused union membership among workers in private industry to shrink by large margins.

After 1970, enrollment numbers for employees joining unions in federal, state, and local governments were back on the rise[20] as the mood favored free competition[21] along with the government deregulation of industries like airlines, trucking, and telephones over the objections of unions.[22]

The 1980s saw one of the most impactful federal involvements in an organized union action when President Ronald Reagan (the only president to ever have been a union leader) ordered the members of the Professional Air Traffic Controllers Union to report to work or lose their jobs and face federal sanctions. The order delivered a major blow to the organized labor movement, and it started the decline of membership that was realized in the latter part of the twentieth century.[23]

The turn of the twenty-first century brought with it new concerns in an emerging technology industry and a continued struggle to strengthen the organized movement in the United States. President George W. Bush pledged to remove collective bargaining rights from nearly two hundred thousand civil servants in the Transportation Security Administration while denying that same right to airport security screening personnel. Also, in the early twenty-first century, President Obama signed the Lilly Ledbetter Fair Pay Act,[24] which restored the rights of working women to sue over pay discrimination.

Leading up to 2020, the number of union members across the United States continued to increase, and some states saw union growth for the first time in decades.[25] Although the total number of union members increased by nearly 2 percent in 2017, union membership often fluctuates yearly due to hiring or layoffs in individual sectors.[26] In recent years, the percentage of individuals in the workforce belonging to unions reached 10.7 percent (2017).[27]

Efforts continue to help enhance protections in the National Labor Relations Act and the Domestic Workers' Bill of Rights in several states. Organized labor continues to work to establish better working conditions and fight for the rights of employees in many industries.

## COACHES CORNER

Educational leaders utilize successful strategies, programs, and policies—in consideration of the needs of personnel—from leaders in other industries and markets. This includes plays used in real estate acquisitions; human resources development; customer service demands; construction needs; and the enhancement of social and emotional learning for employees and stakeholders.

It is important to always have an historical context in consideration of all the systems that surround the role of the educational leader. By learning the struggles that have occurred and respecting the plight of those past leaders across all industries who have worked so hard to help design the landscape of leadership, a leader can advance her school, district, college, university, or organization to a level necessary to be revered by her colleagues across the nation.

As one looks at the successful implementation of strategies and programs from other industry leaders, it is just as (if not more) important to learn and study those strategies and designs that didn't work and were not effective. Taking those failed attempts, a leader knows what needs to be attenuated to turn one leader's failure into another leader's triumph.

## YOU MAKE THE CALL: CASE SCENARIO

Joe Gaba has been a school leader in a neighboring district for the last twenty-two years. During those two decades, he has had many successful school years but has also made several unpopular decisions that have brought negativity to his school system.

Your county association has put Mr. Gaba in charge of the student awards ceremony, and he is looking to change many of the program traditions that have been in place since the awards ceremony was started back in 1995.

Several of your supervisors and teachers learned about the proposed changes to the program, and they are very concerned that the changes will affect your organization and students the most.

What plays do you call?
How do you handle speaking with Mr. Gaba?
How do you handle discussing the situation with your personnel?

## NOTES

1. Madeline Will, "Teachers' Unions Expected Big Membership Losses. Here's Why Those Haven't Panned Out," *Education Week*, June 27, 2019.

2. Bureau of Labor Statistics, Division of Industrial Relations, under the supervision of Harry P. Cohany, chief. Past and present contributors include Theodore W. Reedy, John M. Brumm, Nelson M. Bortz, Witt Bowden, Joseph W. Bloch, and Joseph P. Goldberg of the Bureau of Labor Statistics and Professor Albert A. Blum of Michigan State University (1976).

3. Robert Zieger, *American Workers, American Unions* (Baltimore, MD: John Hopkins University Press, 1994).

4. Ibid.

5. Christopher L. Tomlins, *The State and the Unions: Labor Relations, Law, and the Organized Labor Movement in America, 1880–1960* (New York: Cambridge University Press, 1985).

6. Ibid.

7. Robert H. Zieger and Gilbert J. Gall, *American Workers, American Unions: The Twentieth Century*, 3rd ed. (Baltimore, MD: Johns Hopkins University Press, 2002); Lawrence Richards, *Union-Free America: Workers and Antiunion Culture* (Urbana: Illinois University Press, 2010).

8. Peter R. Shergold, *Working-Class Life: The "American Standard" in Comparative Perspective, 1899–1913* (Pittsburgh, PA: University of Pittsburgh Press, 1982), 5–7, 222.

9. Howard Zinn, *A People's History of the United States* (New York: Harper Perennial Modern Classics, 2005), 256; George Brown Tindall and David E. Shi, *America: A Narrative History*, brief 9th ed., vol. 2 (New York: W. W. Norton, 2012), 590.

10. Tindall and Shi, *America: A Narrative History*, 590.

11. David Montgomery, "Strikes in Nineteenth-Century America," *Social Science History* 4, no. 1 (Winter 1980): 81–104.

12. Ibid.

13. Alice Kessler-Harris, *Gendering Labor History* (Urbana and Chicago: University of Illinois Press, 2007); Alice Henry, Carrie Chapman Catt, and National American Woman Suffrage Association Collection, *The Trade Union Woman* (New York; London: D. Appleton and Company, 1915); N. S. Dye, *As Equal as Sisters* (Columbia, MO: University of Missouri Press, 1980).

14. Lettie Gavin, *American Women in World War I: They Also Served* (Boulder: University Press of Colorado, 2006).

15. Biographical/Historical Collection: Mary van Kleeck papers. Smith College Special Collections.

16. Steve Fraser and Gary Gerstle, eds., *The Rise and Fall of the New Deal Order, 1930–1980* (Princeton, NJ: Princeton University Press, 1990).

17. Taylor E. Dark, *The Unions and the Democrats: An Enduring Alliance* (Ithaca, NY: Cornell University Press, 2001).

18. Bruce Western and Jake Rosenfeld, "Workers of the World Divide," *Foreign Affairs*, April 20, 2012.

19. Susan Margaret Collins, ed., *Imports, Exports, and the American Worker* (Washington, DC: Brookings Institution Press, 1998), 288–90.

20. James T. Bennett and Bruce E. Kaufman, *The Future of Private Sector Unionism in the United States* (Armonk, NY; London: M. E. Sharpe, 2002), 373–78; Zieger and Gall, *American Workers, American Unions: The Twentieth Century*, 3rd ed.; Richards, *Union-Free America*.

21. Martha Derthick and Paul J. Quirk, *The Politics of Deregulation* (Washington, DC: Brookings Institution Press, 1985).

22. Ibid.

23. Herbert R. Northrup, "The Rise and Demise of PATCO," *Industrial and Labor Relations Review* 37, no. 2 (1984): 167–184.

24. On January 29, 2009, President Barack Obama signed into law the Lilly Ledbetter Fair Pay Act. The Act requires employers to redouble their efforts to ensure that their pay practices are nondiscriminatory and to make certain that they keep the records needed to prove the fairness of pay decisions.

25. Arthur Thomas, "Wisconsin Union Membership Grew by 11,000 in 2017," *Milwaukee BizTimes*, January 19, 2018.

26. Lawrence Mishel, "Overall Union Membership Rises in 2017, Union Density Holds Steady," Economic Policy Institute, January 19, 2018.

27. U.S. Bureau of Labor Statistics, Databases, Tables & Calculators by Subject.

*Chapter 4*

# Politics in the Workplace

The culture of any workplace includes specific political overtones that need to be successfully navigated to ensure a positive work environment. Leaders must be able to identify opposing tactics and implement strategies to move their mission forward and generate support from colleagues and subordinates.

It is imperative that the school executive understands that there is a distinct difference between being "political" as opposed to being "politically savvy." Each of these definitions brings with it a plethora of promises and problems in consideration of one's relationship with labor and her workforce. Thus, it is crucial that an individual knows which type of "game plan" is appropriate to use in each and every labor-management situation in order to advance the organization.

### POLITICAL

Terms like *quid pro quo* and *favor* are not foreign to the language of a political operative within any organization. A person who is political may use his power in a position and his contacts to cause a decision to be made or a change to occur in his favor. Most, if not all, of the circumstances surrounding such defined political acts are due to an exchange in favors or the prospect that favors will be exchanged sometime in the future.

Even actions that present themselves based on ensuring that something doesn't occur are considered political in nature. For example, giving someone assistance so that they don't vote a certain way is a very political action. With this "exchange" comes a promise based on an action that carries favor towards a certain specific outcome. Individuals within any political arena utilize tactics in order to create changes through a political lens.

Although this seems like the easy way out and a preferable situation, it is almost inevitable that actions taken that constitute a political means always come back to hurt the individual taking the action at some point in his career.

Simply put, a political favor will be renamed a political liability at some point in the near or distant future.

Whether the original action that was taken will be seen by others in a different time as problematic, or relationships fade as new alliances begin to hover over the political atmosphere, it is important when entering this type of interaction that one is wholly aware that one day, he will be wreaking havoc for the politics that were "played."

With the labor force, besides its own political infrastructure and subculture of leadership values and experiences, a few promises for the simple return of production and sustainability goes a very long way. The educational leader must be extremely careful in obtaining the reasoning behind any political mobility from the labor side, and he may want to seek answers to the following questions before entering into any compromise or discussion:

- What are the repercussions of entering into decisions based on political capital with the employees and their leadership?
- What do both gain from the decisions and the compromises agreed to during the negotiated session?
- What are the drawbacks to agreeing to or denying the decisions based on the politics involved with said planning, or lack thereof?
- What will be the possible "fallout" or ramifications to the political agreements made as personnel changes on both sides of leadership for the organization and the labor force?
- What are some worst- and best-case scenarios with a move this political?

## POLITICALLY SAVVY

The school executive who can be considered and even revered for being politically savvy is by definition an individual who understands the political "landscape," and how any particular move, addition, or attenuation of projects, programs, and protocols affects the organization and its stakeholders both individually and as a whole. More important, being politically savvy means that the individual in question knows how each move or decision affects herself and her overall position in the organization as well.

Being savvy is being smart. This is not to be confused with being "safe" since there are times when even an action that is savvy can be considered dangerous and have a negative impact on an individual's ability to lead and future influences within the organization. An educational executive must work hard to understand all of the "connections" within her organization. This doesn't include only those relationships formed by her leadership team, but the internal and external forces that help establish a pattern of productivity over every area of the organization.

This ability to interpret connections among and between offices, departments, "cliques," and many other relationships that affect the daily work activity of the office is key to ensuring that the executive maintains confidence in controlling any and all potential problems and personal or business conflicts that may arise without him knowing otherwise.

## COACHES CORNER

Any individual who states that politics do not play a role in education is just wrong. Members of both the leader and labor sides of the educational playing field must remain politically savvy, but must refrain from becoming political. There is a very broad and distinct difference between both of these definitions.

First, being politically savvy in an educational setting describes an individual who is grounded and knowledgeable in the landscape of her organization. She knows who her "players" are and is fully aware of their needs and what they represent. A politically savvy executive also knows the value of her relationships with different stakeholder groups and what she needs to sustain in her role as a leader in order to keep those relationships whole and continue to build political capital. Being savvy also means knowing the pulse of her workplace and understanding the needs of her employees.

Being "political" is more like making a direct impact on a situation within the organization. It could come in the form of supporting a particular "side" to get what is needed, or providing a quid pro quo to ensure a solution reveals a certain outcome.

A political leader will always have a part of his constituent base under the impression that his words don't support his actions and vice versa. He may be viewed as a leader who takes advantage of a situation to benefit his own needs and lose any evidence of being genuine if he was caught in a political quagmire.

Unfortunately, at times school executives must use politics in the workplace to provide a specific direction and outcomes for those individuals she represents. And there is the rub. It is impossible for the executive to have every single group supportive of a decision every single time a decision is made. This will always upset certain members of your workforce and labor units.

It is very important for the school executive to understand this simple code to be recited by any individual who sits in a boardroom chair: The board that hires you is rarely ever the board who fires you. Thus, political decisions made, both for and against stakeholders, will always come back to hurt you at some point.

## YOU MAKE THE CALL: CASE SCENARIO

John Liu, the president of the local labor association in your office, just informed you that several of your employees overheard some supervisors discussing that layoffs were coming over the next week. John is furious that you didn't discuss this with him, and the rumors are now causing panic among the working staff.

> What plays would you use?
> In this scenario, there are several issues that will ultimately affect relationships at the workplace.
> What is your first move?
> What will you correct in order to ensure this doesn't occur in future years?
> How will you ensure that the new protocols will occur?

*Chapter 5*

# The Importance of the Labor-Management Relationship

Although there is never any doubt when identifying the need to create a successful and productive culture in the workplace, most important is maintaining a positive relationship with members of your workforce and their representation. It is necessary to disagree in order to ensure an appropriate professional and creative atmosphere; however, at the end of the day, the team must know that the level of respect for all members and positions runs deep and can be witnessed throughout all levels of the organization.

Yes, it is important as well that everyone involved knows that the leader/manager makes the ultimate decisions. Whether right or wrong for the company or organization, the full weight of responsibility, success, and/or failure falls directly on the shoulders of the individual in charge. Regardless, it is imperative that the executive realizes and fully appreciates that she cannot reach any goal or milestone and/or make changes and corrections without the full cooperation and strong work ethic of her labor force.

This all seems relatively obvious. Well, if that is such a true statement, why are there so many disputes that lead to poor relations between labor and management? Simply put, management doesn't fully understand the leverage that its workers and unions have in consideration of production nor does management always know how to successfully utilize that leverage for its own cause.

There are very simple "plays" from the school executive's playbook that can be used to help in creating a successful and positive relationship between labor forces and managers/leaders in any educational system or organization. However, where formulating the successful playbook is simple, selecting and following the right play to create a working and profitable outcome is a whole other consideration that solely depends upon the leader himself and his ability to lead effectively.

## Know the Needed Outcome

The school executive cannot lead the charge in consideration of any important decision without first knowing the outcome she needs to reach and even surpass her established goal. This may include several avenues that outline a plan of action to meet the purpose of the goal that she has set forth for her organization to conquer. In order to formulate a strong relationship and maintain control in directing that relationship accordingly, the demands established must have direction and be clear and concise. It sounds simple, but leaders at times are so "caught up" in a process of "how can I get there" that they forget where they are trying to get to.

## Understand the Needs of Your Employees

Arguably, the most important "plays" designed throughout this entire book will include the executive's need to strengthen his understanding of the needs of his employees. This includes professional as well as personal needs, and (as strange as this sounds) needs that his employee will come to recognize are important in the near and distant future. An example of this may be professional development, training courses or seminars, and possible position changes to help create a crossover approach with job duties or expand roles within the organization.

Understanding the employees and other individuals on the labor side is a major consideration for advancing productivity and meeting the mission that has been set in place. Assisting others through a personal crisis is also a part of that mission. The executive doesn't need to seem "personal" or become involved in the decision making for his employee's family, etc.; however, understanding what is needed and knowing what can be done in a professional sense to help alleviate any stressors or concerns will go a long way in assisting that individual and increasing morale overall.

## Smile

Sounds so simple, right? Unfortunately, it is one of the easiest acts that a successful leader must constantly remind herself to do when looking to consistently strengthen the management-labor relationship. Although an executive may have fifty other pressing thoughts on her mind as she comes in contact with an employee or colleague, the lack of any friendly or cordial gesture can lead to a plethora of issues that may continue to spin out of control.

## Communicate about Issues Often

A good "play" for the school executive to utilize is to communicate with his employees, staff, and constituents often. With media expanding so rapidly and the ease of access to applications in only seconds from any mobile device, there are limited reasons as to why communications could be thwarted or even sometimes nonexistent. An executive can maintain current relationships and enter into new ones through consistent communication among employees.

## "Show" Your Appreciation

The school executive in the education industry doesn't always need to show appreciation only at specific times of the year (holidays, etc.) and through gestures or gifts. Instead, her appreciation towards her labor force can be known through her engaging in friendly conversation with staff; an email or correspondence showing that she appreciates what everyone has accomplished; handwritten notes with accolades in mailboxes or left on desks; and small vocal reminders that the organization works together as one unit.

The executive must be very careful, however, that she is consistent with these shows of appreciation, in that they must be given to all employees equally regardless of personal feelings or perceived institutional value. A leader must always take the "high road" when ensuring that all members of her team feel appreciated and respected.

## Don't Always Hold Meetings during the "Rough" Times

There are many educational leaders who insist on holding weekly, or biweekly meetings to ensure production and communication are in sync with the mission of the organization. It is imperative that meetings are productive and are only held when necessary.

The more meetings become regular events and individuals leave the sessions without valuable or viable information, the more attenuated the executive's role as a true leader becomes and he tends to show more of his managerial prerogative. After following that rule from the playbook, the executive then must be sure to hold meetings or school/department "pow wows" during the good times as well as times when things need correcting.

In other words, if he is quick to schedule a meeting when the pressure is on or mistakes need correcting, he must be just as fast at getting his teams together to give an "atta boy" or accolades for great performance. This is a play that goes a real long way in ensuring that true leadership can be sustainable for the executive, since the labor force will work harder to get through those rough patches when they know an appreciation is still on the horizon after the problems are corrected.

## Never Make Immediate Decisions

A leader's mantra in this area is very simple—Unless someone is literally "on fire," nothing needs to be done immediately! In other words, for 99 percent of the decisions she will make, the executive can take pause, do research, seek counsel, and regroup before she makes a final decision. This is an extremely important skill that an individual needs when "running" each play from the playbook in order to effectively navigate the workplace, politics, and conflicts with personnel and union leadership.

Too many times, leaders make decisions based on emotion or through a reactionary measure due to what is occurring at that actual moment in time. It is most beneficial to the management-labor relationship and in consideration of the respect afforded to the executive herself if she contemplates the pros and cons of every decision and considers the input and needs of all stakeholder groups prior to acting on the matter at hand.

## Sometimes, You Have to Say "Yes"

It is very easy to say "no." Sometimes, you just have to say "yes." One can argue that nearly every successful executive can attribute some portion of his success to taking chances or thinking way outside the proverbial "box." The same holds true for ideas from labor forces, employees, and even subordinate managers who come to him with ideas that have been thought out and supported by other members of the organization. In turn, the leader should support these initiatives to ensure their success since every employee's success measures towards his success as well.

## See the Issue and Its Importance from the Perspective of the Other Side

Whenever conflict arises, it is extremely necessary and beneficial to understand the opposing perspective in order to reach some type of compromise or to even win the argument outright. Further, the executive must realize how important the issue is to those who are raising it and what effect the outcome (whatever it may be) will have on members of the organization. This can only occur if the executive understands what the other argument is and what political capital may be gained or lost in consideration of her decision.

## Utilize Data to Support Your Point/Argument

Whenever an executive intends to challenge or dispute something put forth by workers, constituents, or members of other stakeholder groups, he must have data or evidence to support his point and make his argument. This can come in the form of past practice, data sets, or other research that he intends to utilize to support his position and why he is making the decision at hand.

The more relevant the data, the better the argument for supporting the executive's position over any other. It's true that the executive really doesn't have to have any reason to decide the way he chooses to; however, it is crucial that he maintains the support of his team members and can do this by showing how he came to make the decision he did.

## Always Appreciate the Dialogue

Regardless of a positive or negative interaction when in the process of building the management-labor relationship, the school executive must always appreciate that the communication lines are open. When critical dialogue cannot be fostered between an executive and his workforce, the absence of communication can cause major damage to an already established relationship and greatly delay the start of a new one.

Further, all conversations must remain cordial and include a mutual respect between all parties. It is "ok" to raise voices at times, but overall, the conversation should be seen as fair and engaging for all sides.

## Make Sure Your Counterpart (and the Team) Feels Somewhat Empowered After a Dispute

Whether the school executive is negotiating terms with labor/union leadership or she is engaged in a dispute with her entire team, it is her duty to ensure all sides come out of the compromise feeling empowered. Regardless of who "wins," a true leader can always find ways that everyone involved reaps some type of benefit from the exchange of ideas that has just occurred.

Empowering others through feeling a true sense of accomplishment ensures that the lines of communication remain open. This is extremely important for future issues that may be more complicated or time-consuming than the issue in question. By laying a framework now, it is easier to work together when stalemates seem inevitable or the leader-labor relationship is strained.

## When/If Possible, Offer More than Expected

After a dispute, negotiation, or a compromise, both the executive and his workforce will review the process that had occurred and how each "side" fared in getting what each was hoping to achieve. If possible, the executive should consider giving more of what was asked by his workforce than requested.

Here, he is causing a paradigm shift, in that the expectation of compromising for the minimum "ask" is overshadowed by what now is seen as a generous gesture from management. This doesn't always need to be monetary in value, and it can even include language changes to processes that make protocols for workers more attainable.

## COACHES CORNER

Educational leadership is an extremely important field for ensuring a productive management-labor relationship. Regardless of union association, an administrative team's respect, admiration, direction, development, and support of its labor force is crucial to the production of successful markers of growth for students and citizens alike. An executive's tone and constructive measures must effectuate such a change in her staff that it permeates to her students as well.

In consideration of working alongside union leadership, the measure of a successful relationship and its positive impact on the organization only occurs if mutual respect is maintained by both sides. It must be wholly understood that there will be arguments and disagreements most days, but they are business in nature—never personal. An executive has reached the apex of his administrative career when he can easily separate and identify both of those mindsets. Seeking retribution or retaliation for differences and actions will only create greater dissention and thwart any positive progress.

Instead, the executive must work on this relationship like any with a significant other—full of "gives" and more "gives." The takeaways are the progress you will make together for the betterment of the personnel in your workforce, your students, and the school or college/university community.

## YOU MAKE THE CALL: CASE SCENARIO

After an announcement you just made of a program that your organization is introducing, Maggie Simmons, one of your supervisors, approaches you and explains that several of your employees are upset because when you thanked members of the team, you forgot to include their names.

- What plays do you use?
- Besides the immediate issue at hand, what other types of "damage control" will you need to consider to move forward?
- What are your plays moving forward to ensure that a scenario like this is avoided in the future?

*Chapter 6*

# Labor Laws[1]

Although labor relations laws differ among states, there are several federal laws, programs, and protocols that must be acknowledged and followed in order to lead a successful business or organization. It is imperative that executives in both blue- and white-collar industries comprehend how these laws relate to company policies and can create issues within the workforce and the organization.

There are over 180 federal laws enforced by the United States Department of Labor that protect employees at their workplaces across the nation. The following lists and summarizes several of the more prominent statutes that affect businesses, organizations, and the workforce.[2]

## Wages and Hours

Known as the Fair Labor Standards Act, it requires employers to pay their employees (who are not otherwise exempt) at least the federal minimum wage and overtime pay of one-and-one-half times the regular rate of pay.

The act restricts hours that children under age sixteen (unless the job is agricultural in nature) can work and does not permit employment for individuals younger than eighteen in certain jobs that are considered "dangerous." Children working in agricultural positions who are sixteen years or younger cannot work during regular school hours.

## Workplace Safety and Health

From furniture to air quality, mold and asbestos, the Occupational Safety and Health (OSH) Act regulates safety and health conditions in private industries and those employers considered public sector. Compliance with the Occupational Safety and Health Administration's (OSHA's) regulations and safety and health standards ensures that employers provide their employees with a workplace that is free from any recognized, serious hazards. The law is enforced through workplace inspections and appropriate safety investigations.

### Unions and Their Members

The Labor-Management Reporting and Disclosure Act of 1959[3] covers the relationship between a union and its members. In turn, the act protects union funds and promotes union democracy by requiring organized labor unions to file annual reports and other disclosures. It is a system of checks and balances put in place to ensure the fiduciary responsibility of unions to their membership.

### Employee Protection (Whistleblower)

Whistleblower protections for employees are enforced through OSHA and are established to protect employees from retaliation and sanctions after reporting violations.

### Uniformed Services Employment and Reemployment Rights Act

Individuals who serve in the armed forces, reserves, or National Guard have rights to maintain employment with the employer they were with when they entered the service. Thank you, veterans!

### Family and Medical Leave Act

The Family and Medical Leave Act (FMLA) requires employers to give up to twelve weeks of unpaid, job-protected leave to eligible employees (in businesses or organizations with at least fifty employees) for the birth of their child, adoption, or serious illness of the employee herself, her spouse, child, or parent.

### Government Contract Awards

First, the Davis-Bacon Act requires the paying of a prevailing wage and benefits to employees of all contractors who are engaged in federal government construction projects. Next, the McNamara-O'Hara Service Contract Act sets wage rates and other labor standards for employees of contractors providing professional services to the federal government. Finally, payment of minimum wages by contractors who may be providing materials and supplies to the federal government is covered under the Walsh-Healey Public Contracts Act.

### Migrant and Seasonal Agricultural Workers

The Migrant and Seasonal Agricultural Worker Protection Act provides parameters in consideration of the hiring and work-related activities of agricultural employers, farm labor contractors, and any association that is using migrant and seasonal agricultural workers. The Act outlines wage protections, housing and transportation safety standards, and contractor disclosure requirements.

## COACHES CORNER

Educational leaders must ensure that they have a strong human resources team as part of their leadership council in order to provide both employees and the leaders themselves with appropriate guidance in consideration of changes and updates to labor laws and protocols. Further, it is important that the leader ensures her workforce is educated and kept current on their rights and responsibilities.

As laws do constantly change and are applied differently to specific situations, it is absolutely imperative that the leader consults with legal counsel prior to making any personnel changes that may affect employment or placement.

## YOU MAKE THE CALL: CASE SCENARIO

Mrs. Ferrara requests to have a meeting with you to discuss her taking a leave of absence to take care of her mother who just fell and broke her hip.

What plays would you call?
Knowing that she has release time available, how do you navigate company policy, federal law, and upholding morale based on this sequence of events?
What other employees/departments would you involve in the discussion and decision?

## NOTES

1. Summary of the Major Laws of the Department of Labor, U.S. Department of Labor (2021).

2. The summary of federal statutes dealing with labor is intended for informational and recognition purposes. Any references or strategic decisions made with regard to these laws should only be done after seeking advice from legal counsel.

3. Also known as the Landrum-Griffin Act.

*Chapter 7*

# Labor Defined among Industries

Many educational leaders across the nation lead in districts and educational systems that include labor unions and associations that organize employees to enhance working conditions and contractual agreements. In many of these cases, the educational organizations become linked with those organized units in other industries and maintain the direction and labor paradigm as established by those industries.

Labor forces are the backbone and foundation of many industries. Each industry has a history of the labor movement specific to the progress and growth (or loss) of said industry, and there is a specific outline and characterization for each classification of worker and how they have influenced that industry throughout the years to these current times.

Without a strong and independent workforce behind a product or service, any industry becomes weak and competition runs low, which leads to less of an incentive to enhance quality and technology that will better the lives of humankind.

In certain industries, labor unions have worked with management as a necessity to improve working conditions for employees to ensure industry standards are at maximum potential and workers are compensated a fair wage based on the production output that they are certifying for their company.

In earlier times, management and executive leadership took advantage of individuals with a lack of education based on their need to earn some type of wage to support their family. Labor unions created the necessary shift that showed how those executives and owners of companies throughout specific industries would only be as successful as they were because of the hard work of such a dedicated workforce.

Thus, once incentives were formalized and industry leaders started to care about the mental health and physical wellness of their workers, the paradigm shifted from minimal or steady production to enhanced business strategies and exponential growth in consideration of company value, human capital, and product recognition. One can even make a good argument that when the needs of the labor movement—throughout each specific industry—are finally addressed, an immediate and absolute "spike" in productivity and performance should be realized.

In fact, even though every industry may not include some type of official and organized labor union or professional association to support and represent the professionals and workers in a particular company or a specific field, it takes some type of representative body or an individual who is a liaison between management and workers to advance said office, factory, school district, restaurant, etc. into the next tier of profits and public notoriety.

Although one can add hundreds of valuable checkpoints to act as benchmarks for identifying the defined scope and sequence of what workers are expected to do, labor is defined among industries from the inclusion of two distinct categories in nearly every field. First, how does the workforce support productivity in the industry, and second, would the industry fail without ample support from labor?

Overall, each specific industry has a specialized labor force and most have organized unions and associations to assist workers with negotiating conditions, pay, and welfare. Although the general mission is established based on the tenets of the leader-worker relationship at large, some industries have specialized needs and plans of action in order to protect workers and maintain productive working environments. Some of this includes the following:

### Manufacturing and Innovation

Manufacturing and the creation of innovative tools for trades is a backbone industry for exporting textiles and other goods to a global marketplace. Included in nearly every business-related service, the manufacturing of goods and the production of items to help enhance living through advances in technology is an important component in consideration of the management-labor relationship.

> Labor Union Presence: Strong
> Support from Management: Necessary to ensure production of items in a timely manner
> Main Issues/Concerns: Working conditions; wages and benefits; job security

### Retail

The purchasing and selling of goods to consumers for consumption and entertainment purposes was a $5.5 trillion industry in 2020. Retail serves as a catalyst industry since it relies ultimately on other industries to produce goods, transport items, etc.

Labor Union Presence: Medium
Support from Management: Management is very involved in daily routine of workforce
Main Issues/Concerns: Working conditions; hours; salary/minimum wage; fringe benefits

## Construction

Construction is undoubtedly a labor-intensive industry. Although a construction job includes many tendrils (legal, architectural, manufacturing, etc.) to support the project, the backbone of the industry entails workers and laborers with different skill sets.

Labor Union Presence: Strong
Support from Management: Medium
Main Issues/Concerns: Working conditions; hours; union labor; prevailing wages; job security/insurance from work stoppages and layoffs

## Finance

A white-collar industry, financial experts and members of a business team/office make up the fiscal backbone of any company or organization.

Labor Union Presence: Very low
Support from Management: Medium (workers are self-producers)
Main Issues/Concerns: Contract wages; fringe benefits

## Education

There are more than three million teachers who supervise students in K–12 classrooms in the United States. Some of the strongest unions in the country are educator affiliated, and these individuals arguably shape, build, and produce the most important widget of all—the future adults of tomorrow.

Labor Union Presence: Very Strong
Support from Management: High
Main Issues/Concerns: Working conditions; work hours; wages; benefits

## Agriculture

An industry that has been witness to many changes over the decades, but still is an essential component of imported and exported perishable goods to retail chains and other producers, the agricultural workforce has benefited from the genesis of specific technologies and government subsidy.

> Labor Union Presence: Low
> Support from Management: Low
> Main Issues/Concerns: Commodity growth; weather patterns; wages

## Transportation

The transportation industry is imperative to the delivery of goods and items to and from suppliers and retail store owners across the country and around the world.

> Labor Union Presence: Very Strong
> Support from Management: Medium
> Main Issues/Concerns: Working conditions; hours; fee structure

## Health Care

Individuals in health care settings represent a workforce that faces many regulatory factors and very difficult working hazards/conditions.

> Labor Union Presence: Minimal
> Support from Management: Strong
> Main Issues/Concerns: Working conditions; shifts; wages

## Mining

Another American "backbone" industry, mining companies created entire communities around worksites to ensure production of coal and minerals would benefit both business and personal consumption.

> Labor Union Presence: Medium
> Support from Management: Medium
> Main Issues/Concerns: Working conditions; hours; health and safety

## Research

Research and design permeate every industry and affect individuals in nearly every aspect of their daily lives. Without research, products and services cannot be improved, which enhances the quality of life for all persons.

>Labor Union Presence: None
>Support from Management: Minimal; researchers are independent
>Main Issues/Concerns: Contract wages

## Food Industry

As both a retail and service provider, food can be viewed as the industry that everyone has in common. Thus, it becomes territorial in nature with regard to quality, theme, service, and atmosphere in consideration of where a successful culinarian leads by industry standard.

>Labor Union Presence: Minimal
>Support from Management: Strong
>Main Issues/Concerns: Working conditions; hours/shifts

## Sales

The sales force is a dog-eat-dog industry where individuals work for profits on a commission basis or flat hourly standard. Stakes are high and the environment can be stressful, with the selling of a product or service depending on product placement, quality, and brand recognition. Sales representatives usually have quotas to meet on a monthly basis.

>Labor Union Presence: Medium
>Support from Management: Strong
>Main Issues/Concerns: Wages vs. commission; hours; fringe benefits

## Entertainment

The entertainment industry includes individuals ranging from paid musicians to box office actors to major league baseball players. Individuals that are considered famous within this industry are usually afforded protections through agents and legal counsel.

>Labor Union Presence: Strong
>Support from Management: Tenuous at times

Main Issues/Concerns: Contract; personal interests met

**Public Service**

Those individuals who risk their lives in the line of duty as police and fire personnel and other government officials work within an industry which has federal prohibitions on certain actions and contractual obligations.

Labor Union Presence: Strong
Support from Management: Strong
Main Issues/Concerns: Wages; shifts/hours; health and safety protections

## COACHES CORNER

It is important for educational leaders to examine the strategies for labor relations and personnel needs of leaders from successful companies in other industries. These can be systems on national and global scales as well as leaders of businesses and companies local to the educational system or the leaders' home areas.

There are many general crossover skills and applications for educational leaders to utilize that are not industry specific. Some of these include how a leader deals with confrontation and retains employees and workers. Regardless of what is produced by a specific industry or what service is fulfilled, the level of productivity and desired outcome remains the same for the leader/manager of any organization.

Once again, it is important for a leader in an educational system to study the actions of managers and labor leaders in other industries in order to strengthen his relationships within his own system with his own employees and leadership team. There is much to be learned from those individuals who deal with the tenets of organizational leadership as it pertains to systems dealing with individuals and their productivity.

One understands that overall, no one likes to admit that educational systems aren't "run" as a business; however, leaders and chief executives who are in the field understand that the complex relationship between budget and production is as important in education as it is in any other major industry that exists today. One may argue that the complexities are even more intense in education since the private, public, and government sectors overlap in all areas that the school executive needs to navigate throughout the workplace.

## YOU MAKE THE CALL: CASE SCENARIO

Aaron Decker Jonas is a supervisor who reveals that several workers from a neighboring school system have inquired about openings. Over the last several months, three retirements in two departments have left scheduling difficult in consideration of meeting contractual obligations as well as your auditors claiming your budget lines are depleting since you are paying for coverages.

What calls do you make?
How do you enhance recruitment?
How do you involve stakeholders and to what extent?

*Chapter 8*

# Leading Together

Meaningful leadership includes facilitating and sharing the commitment of progress with other members of the team, especially between workers who share the same vision and goal. It is crucial for leaders and managers to really understand that success cannot be achieved and celebrated without positive input and strong production from each and every member involved with the company or organization.

Too many times, the school executive and/or her leadership team take credit for the success of the organization. Naturally, there are many accolades to be gained and given to those individuals in the "top" positions of any organizational hierarchy who continue to move the mission of that organization forward in every possible area.

Through the leader's vision for the organization, his ability to formulate a powerful team, and the consistent strengthening of research and design relative to a product or a particular service, a leader in the workforce is tasked with developing the perfect playbook for success, and therefore should be credited with such an impressive outlook on the performance of the company.

However, it would just be unreasonable for any leader—or any individual for that matter—to ever believe that any goal can be reached without the full support of and respect from the labor force of that organization. To do so would be not only a big mistake, but detrimental to the overall morale and production value of the company or organization.

Therefore, it is overly imperative that an executive ensures that the management and labor sides are seen as leading together in order to help effectuate any and all changes that are needed to move the mission forward. This may seem to be an easy and undaunting task. On the contrary, the ability of both management and labor to lead together can easily become lopsided and off-track due to egos, unpredictable differences, and unreasonable demands—from both sides.

One issue includes the changing of "players" on both sides where union workforces hold elections and executives sometimes come and go. Other deterrents include inexperienced personnel and major differences of opinion. Regardless of the immediate concerns, it is the mission of the executive to create a bridge between herself and the workforce leaders in order to steady the course and continue productivity.

The executive's playbook includes plays and strategies he can use to help fortify the relationship between teams:

## Help Strengthen the Leadership of Labor Teams

The executive can help strengthen the leadership of her organization's labor leadership teams by offering professional development opportunities in several leadership areas. Also, by hosting retreats and/or joint development seminars, both entities can work to become a stronger, single unit which will only grow production and advance the vision of the company or organization as a whole.

## Build Positive Morale

By building a deeper, positive morale in and around the workplace, the leadership intensity will exponentially increase as members of the entire team feel less pressured but more obligated to perform job-oriented tasks at a higher efficiency rate. Where a good portion of an individual's day is spent at the workplace, she does not want to remain part of an intrusive, hostile, or poor environment with individuals she doesn't respect. Of course, in a workplace resting high on positive morale the positive environment extends to every area of production, workflow, healthy living, and emotional awareness.

## From Garbage Cans to Private Jets

It doesn't matter who is doing what job—what matters is if the job is being done right. In any play, each player is charged with a specific duty or task, and if each individual executed his part correctly, the team would score each and every time. Every individual employee, supervisor, staff member, etc. is no more or no less important than any other individual in the system.

All the way from the custodian who empties the garbage daily to the executive traveling back-and-forth from city to city on a private jet, each individual in a company or organization has a purpose, and together the purpose meets the definition of success. Specific to education, leaders on both the management and labor sides must lead together for the purpose of ensuring that everyone in the system understands their importance to the mission and how much they are appreciated.

## Thank the Team Often

Who doesn't like to hear a sincere, heartfelt "thank you" every now and then? The executive play here is that the thankfulness must be genuine. It must come just at the perfect time . . . when it is least expected! It's impossible for an executive to thank individuals or groups too much; however, it cannot seem coached, rehearsed, or "fake" in any way.

## "I Am Not Responsible, but I Am to Blame"

The executive's credo. At any given moment, a member of the workforce in an organization can be doing something that is detrimental to the organization without the executive's knowledge or approval. Regardless of who is responsible for any such action, mistake, or mistreatment, there is truly only one person to take blame. Learning to lead together means that an executive needs to gracefully accept this fate, and work to right the wrongs and correct the mistakes that are made.

## Be Human and Realistic

The most important play for the executive who is learning to lead with others is that she must be human. She must always understand the hierarchy of individual needs as it pertains to each individual member of the organization. A humanistic approach to problem solving, workplace engagement, and establishing partnerships will solidify the executive's role in the organization and facilitate a commitment towards progress from the labor workforce. By showing individuals they are cared for and that their needs are understood, there is no stopping the initiatives and benchmarks that can be met in the near and distant future.

## COACHES CORNER

Education courses, professional development, seminars, etc. always reference leadership. Lifelong learners become leaders by utilizing their knowledge and skills to help others reach and surpass their ultimate potential in consideration of their own needs and the needs of the school, students, and institution.

School executives help to create leaders among their labor force by providing opportunities for their teams to take courses for advanced degrees, facilitating clubs to spotlight their interests, and providing lateral opportunities for staff to assist others in supervisory or advisory roles. Leading together is the only way to ensure that an educational system will reach the pinnacle of success in more than one area that is important to students, faculty, staff, and all related constituent groups. It is important for the executive to always remember that disagreements will occur, but the path of least resistance that is layered in compromise and understanding will make everyone successful and foster a positive experience for learners.

At times, an executive must put his pride aside and take the "high road" when setting a foundation for compromise to reach a decision that will benefit all interested parties. This type of leadership will give others the opportunity to ensure that there will always be a way to "join" the team where everyone can benefit from the ideas, strengths, and consideration from everyone who will be affected by the choices made.

## YOU MAKE THE CALL: CASE SCENARIO

You were just notified that your system/district has been spotlighted as one of the top five in the region. This will fare well with your board and stakeholders.

What plays will you call?
How will you ensure to involve all stakeholder and constituent groups?

*Chapter 9*

# Power

Power is priceless.

On its face, that statement can sound very conceited. It can also be taken in such a way as to expect that an individual, who has "power" behind her performance, has an ability to persuade others that streams past any unknown barrier.

Power, if used properly in consideration of an organization's labor force and an executive's ability to effectively navigate the workplace, politics, and conflicts with personnel and labor leaders, can be the greatest tool that can be utilized from the executive's "playbook."

Power is the ability of one individual or entity to direct or influence another. An executive's plight includes building a power base and then ensuring to utilize that base to his advantage. It is imperative that the leader monitors how his influence is being monitored by his employees or those individuals whom he leads. The proper balance of power used is important to sustain the advantage that is obtained from the power that is recognized at the onset of the labor-leader relationship.

As one continues to advance his role as manager into becoming a true leader who envisions the future of the organization, he will ultimately face barriers that influence his actions when dealing with employees and programs. These barriers are both internal and external in nature, and where a manager can navigate these influences in real time, a strong leader looks to push through these barriers to dominate the narrative.

**External Barriers as Influencers**

- Power differential too big—Leaders must understand where the political and stakeholder pressures may be stemming from and plan accordingly. Knowing that an outside influence may be too much to "handle" should

lead the executive to pause any plan of action that may create a major conflict and power "struggle" between herself and outside entities.
- Different goals and objectives, priorities—Leaders must ensure that all goals are valued and use directed informational leadership to lead the team or organization and gain power over any external influences.
- Incompatible measures and rewards—Sometimes, outside influencers are examining different quantifiable results than are being used on the inside. The inability to compare "apples to apples" can create a barrier for an executive since data can easily be skewed to insist on a specific outcome or result.
- Rivalry, competitiveness, jealousy—Try to avoid outside competition and political influence as much as possible. It is very difficult to keep track of the power influencers that are part of any external means. Thus, an executive never truly knows the extent and reach of the power that makes up the external barriers.

## Internal Barriers as Influencers

- Lack of knowledge about how to influence—A newer school executive may lack the knowledge base and experience to successfully leverage the power she has gained through her positive interactions with her team. Patience and consistent communication with stakeholder groups, labor leadership, and an organization's workforce is integral to a successful power play for any school executive or leader.
- Blinding attitudes—At times, there will be egos to feed and empathy to be delivered. Although this is extremely important for morale, which leads to a strengthening of power for an organization executive/leader, the needs of your labor force must not be mistaken for the wants of individuals who have set an agenda to attenuate the foundation established by the leader.
- Fear of reactions—A school executive who is fearful or worried about the reactions of her team members is destined to become unsuccessful. Further, the easiest way to lose a strong power base is to let others know that their reactions affect one's ability to lead effectively. Rather, the executive can overcome the barrier by accepting that she has made the best decision she could make for her employees and the organization as a whole based on the information with which she was presented.

The school executive should enter every decision with the understanding that she can absolutely not make everyone happy. However, through explanation, guidance, and additional empathy individuals will have the ability to accept the decision even though they may not agree with it.

- Inability to focus on one's own needs and benefits to others—A major internal barrier to growing power is the leader's inability to recognize and cultivate the need to take care of himself. It's as simple as the airplane rule for oxygen masks. As we all recall the flight attendant's safety instructions at the start of the flight, in the event that the cabin loses pressure . . . an oxygen mask will drop down to assist the passenger with breathing.

Well, as a parent, our first instinct is to protect our children in a crisis situation. But in this case, following that first step may cause the passenger to put himself in danger of "passing out," which would negate any possible assistance for the child. Hence, the passenger must put his own mask on first prior to assisting any child. The same applies for an individual leader, and her own ability to reflect on her actions and the outcomes of these decisions. This process will allow her to continue to grow, strengthen her influence, and ensure that she maintains a healthy reflection on what has occurred.[1]

Power must be utilized correctly to formulate change, enhance performance, and advance productivity throughout any industry or organization. Those individuals in leadership roles on both management and labor sides are most successful when they use their power and positions wisely and in consideration of the task at hand and the goals set forth by the organization.

There have been warehouses of books authored with "power" as a theme. Power can be defined in several different ways in consideration of the industry, method, and manner for which it is used. It is crucial for any leader to understand what parameters are set forth where their power and influence over members in their local organization and more at large within their career or industry is concerned.

Although power can sometimes be seen as synonymous to influence, it can also be extremely dangerous if it is not used correctly. Power is an established way that an individual can control someone or something, and most often to his benefit. To have that ability over the actions and decisions of workers or an industry is a direct way to solidify a necessary position within your organization.

## COACHES CORNER

An educational leader is an individual who can wield an incredible amount of influence over a labor force, her constituents, and an entire community.

Utilized appropriately and in a manner sufficient enough to suggest that the continued work of the executive and her team will continue to move the system forward, power can be magnified and attenuated to meet the demands of the executive and her mission.

Power is a tool to be used to benefit the executive in order to move the entire academic system in the right direction. Usually aligned with political capital and a leader's ability to leverage the power she may have to persuade the outcome of a situation or condition, if utilized correctly power can be used to advance the academic prowess, productivity, morale, and overall rating of an educational institution, school district, charter, or higher education system.

The reasoning behind this is simple—power represents the influence that a leader maintains over her labor force and constituent base. The greater the influence, the greater the level of power that can be used to make a difference.

In an educational community, it is important that the executive and her leadership team provide some authority for faculty and employees within the workplace. Since there are other subordinate groups that are part of the landscape, this type of authority places the onus on other members of the educational system, which may lead to substantial growth in many areas pertinent to student and labor success.

This growth will be evident in academic, social, and personal areas of development. It is important that all individuals charged with effectuating change throughout the system have the ability to grow as leaders through the utilization of power and methods utilized to attain the appropriate gains in standard areas necessary for success.

## YOU MAKE THE CALL: CASE SCENARIO

Frank Scalese is the head negotiator for the new union contract that you have been working on for the last several months. You consider Frank an extremely valuable and loyal employee and colleague, and negotiations have been steadying, which you really appreciate. During the latest compromise, you found that Frank had made a major mistake with one of the benefits packages that could be detrimental to his position as labor leader but will provide incredible savings for you and the system.

> What plays do you call?
> Consider your moral, ethical, and legal obligations with respect to an issue like this during a time of crisis.

## NOTE

1. A. R. Cohen and D. L. Bradford, "Influence Without Authority: The Use of Alliances, Reciprocity, and Exchange to Accomplish Work," *Organizational Dynamics* 17, no. 3 (2002).

*Chapter 10*

# Negotiating to Win

The chapter title seems very matter of fact, no? What else would one be negotiating for if it wouldn't be "to win"? As the school executive works to build and expand his playbook and begins to formulate sequences of "plays" that he will use whenever a situation arises, he learns quickly that every play he has executed correctly will lead him to meet his goal. At times, negotiating a compromise or parts of a contract includes concessions and demands that may seem to come at a loss to the leadership team.

Regardless, if the play sequence is being established to "set up" the final strike at getting to where he needs both himself and his organization to be, then the victory is indicative of the future success he will have in navigating the workplace.

School executives and educational administrators must have strong negotiating skills when dealing with both the day-to-day operations of the workplace and the long-term goals established to ensure a prosperous future. Successful leaders on both the management and labor sides must also secure the tools necessary to negotiate contracts and other productivity demands for the company and individuals they represent.

If a leader feels that negotiating is not an extremely important skill or one skill that can maybe take a "back seat," then leading an organization or company may not be for that individual. Those who negotiate must know how to negotiate "to win." Understandably, those individuals who know how to negotiate successfully realize that winning is symbiotic with compromise when dealing with negotiable terms.

Both the management and labor "sides" coming together for a purposeful outcome is the best situation that any individual could ask for. In fact, one can argue that the compromise is the actual win, since no true and fierce adversary would concede to conditions without gaining something in return. A good—no, a great negotiator—knows this is a victory.

Then if negotiating a win equals a compromise, what is so important in consideration of the labor-management relationship? Simply stated, it's all about the process of getting to that compromise. Call it posturing, call it "games," call it what you will. The fact of the matter is that each successful negotiation strengthens the effective manner in which the next negotiation starts.

Transformational leadership by any distributive means is all about working to a compromise. Through directed informational standards, a leader begins each action with a goal that she already has a preferred answer to. Including stakeholders in the organization is the only way to secure true buy-in for the goal while projecting onus on each of the other members in the organization. Then, the executive can negotiate the terms necessary to meet or surpass the stated objective and always come out ahead of what she thought would be the outcome.

## COACHES CORNER

Educational leaders are constantly negotiating terms, contracts, and other academic and program needs with their faculty, administration, parent, and other community stakeholder groups. The daily negotiations that take place provide a formidable give-and-take in order for the system to live, breathe, and grow substantially while developing best practices that include input and feedback from real constituent groups.

By listening to his labor force and labor leadership, the educational executive maintains the purpose of controlling the outcome based on his ability to involve others in the decision-making processes used to come to the agreement. Using this type of directed informational leadership style, he gains true perspective on negotiating to win even though he may "give up" some ground.

Educational leaders, executives, and administrators alike must be very careful not to allow pride and stubbornness to overshadow the end goal for the task or mission at hand. At times, leaders tend to feel that negotiating terms that seem to benefit the workforce weaken the managerial position of the educational system and will affect learners. On the contrary, inviting teachers, employees, staff, and other members of the labor force to "the table" in negotiating situations is the only way to strengthen the delivery of the mission and the action plans established to meet the goals.

Let's face it—without any say or benefit from a task that one is to provide, why would he or she provide it successfully? Yes, salary and other benefits are an incentive, but as research has shown, leadership must fulfill other needs to ensure that constituents and employees feel successful and important in any organization. As these needs include job security, safety, and other motivating factors leading to self-actualization, a greater need is for an individual teacher, administrator, or staff member to feel empowered to make decisions and negotiate outcomes that benefit the individual employee.

Remember, there are many ways to "win" in an education system. This playbook outlines many methods and strategies for executives who are moving through the day-to-day operations of the workplace, looking to make immediate, short-, and long-term decisions that affect employees and the organization as a whole. Getting the team onboard and working together for the good of the entire system is the "win" the executive must be working towards. Negotiating to ensure that all groups are represented and feel like an important part of the final outcome is the way to get there.

## YOU MAKE THE CALL: CASE SCENARIO

Yolanda Goetz is one of your top staff members who has worked with the system for several years and is in charge of all personnel items in the human resources department. Although she doesn't have supervisory experience or actual duties as outlined by your other unit supervisors and managers in the field, you depend on her to act as a liaison between employee and management issues in consideration of administrative tasks that deal with many areas of human resources.

You have heard that with the experience she has gathered over the last several years, she is being recruited by a neighboring organization that knows of her work ethic and her ability to enhance the performance and morale of your employees and individual teams.

Yolanda has called you and has requested a meeting to discuss some "personal issues" that she has.

- What plays do you make?
- What plays do you prepare for?
- Is Yolanda an employee that you benefit from and will you be prepared to offer some extension of her employment? What BATNA (best alternative to a negotiated agreement) categories would you prepare if this is a possibility?

*Chapter 11*

# Contracts, Agreements, "Handshakes," and Past Practice

There are many types of industry-specific contracts and agreements between labor and management, and each affects production, the organization, and its individual members in different ways. A "deeper dive" into negotiation strategy and tactics of both management and personnel leadership transcends the ideal that fostering good, positive relationships is the only tried-and-true method of ensuring that every and all agreements are met in a timely and productive manner.

Consequently, there are not many industries and organizations that choose not to formally memorialize agreement terms with labor units and/or individual employees. At minimum, these contracts outline the contract duration; compensation; working conditions; time on task; and other employee benefits. A contractual agreement works to hold both management and labor accountable for work production and relief sought to help ensure fair business practices are aligned with expectations of leadership. This could stem from policies created by a board or the directives from a chief executive.

This, of course, is what makes a contract so important—the simple fact that every facet of productivity is "laid out" in some type of codified exhibit so that no executive, team member, or labor leader is taken by surprise or can argue the tenets of the scope and sequence of the "job" as prescribed by the agreement. Sounds good, right?

On the contrary, the outline of the employment agreement still at times needs to be clarified as the impact of actions by the organization's leadership may be perceived as challenging to the labor side. Even though the parameters may seem to be "spelled out" in a specific fashion, the interpretation is something that always keeps each "side" honest with the other. In "creeps" the term *past practice.*

Past practice is defined as any long-standing, frequent practice that is accepted and has been known about by the union and management beforehand. A practice of this nature that meets the standards of past practice is considered to be part of the negotiated contract.[1]

A school executive or member of the management team who attempts to end or enforce a change to a past practice can be subject to grievance provisions as established by the currently enforced contractual agreement. Most often, the practice cannot be attenuated or removed without negotiating the impact of the change with the union membership or their association. This usually occurs in the form of an amendment or can only occur when the next cycle of negotiations occurs.

Protections for past practice can benefit both sides, however. Usually, when textbooks and business/leadership courses discuss past practice and arbitration law, they tend to sway to the labor side. This most often occurs since executives and managers may change a specific type of working condition that becomes the new expectation for employees throughout the course of the day or work cycle. Then, when it no longer benefits the administrative needs of the company or organization, leadership demands a return to what was originally negotiated.

Understandably, this type of insertion of a change can be used maliciously and to the detriment of the workforce. Most often, conditions surrounding these types of "handshake" agreements turn into past practice where the methods continue to occur years after inception of the original change.

Sometimes, these practices are requested by labor units and do work out in management's favor. For example, changes to shift work or preparing reports, etc. that were attenuated to assist workers at one point and have been agreed to by management may not be beneficial to newer employees or those same individuals as other factors may change.

There are several scenarios that illustrate some of the most common uses of past practice in consideration of the workplace and management-labor relations.[2]

## Ambiguous Language

Language in a contract or negotiated agreement may seem clear when the contract is first settled, but more uncertain as time goes by. This especially holds true if a clause has remained in a contract over several years and employees have changed along with the needs of the workforce. Take for example a clause which provides for "premium pay for work over eight hours in a day."

Is an employee entitled to premium pay when her regular shift ends at midnight and the "overtime" occurs on the following day? Is a day defined as a calendar day or as the twenty-four-hour period following the start of a shift? Again, this may have been clear during the original negotiation but now stands as an ambiguous definition.

## General Contract Language

Even simple definitions can cause concerns. For example, what actually constitutes "just cause" and "proper" discipline under the agreement for one executive may be defined differently for another.

## Modifying Apparently Unambiguous Language

Very common in contracts that affect labor relations is language and circumstances that are ambiguous in nature. Let's suppose a union labor contract for a school custodian defines a work day as eight hours, with an unpaid lunch hour of one-half hour. However, employees from this department have consistently worked a straight eight hours with a paid lunch break incorporated within that time. Can the school executive now just abolish the paid meal break?

Further, for a past practice to be binding and enforceable, most judges and arbitrators will hold that the practice must incorporate the following:[3]

- *Clarity and Consistency:* The conduct that considers the past practice must be clearly defined. It must also be viewed as the "invariable response" to a given set of specific conditions.
- *Acceptability:* Management and employees alike must have actual knowledge that the practice exists and accept it as the means of dealing with the situation in question. In other words, it is not a procedure that takes place only when supervision is relaxed or ignored; rather, it is customary to the workplace.
- *Unchanged Underlying Circumstances:* A practice that may be established only due to the result of a particular set of special or underlying circumstances is no broader than those actual circumstances.
- *Mutuality:* The practice must be a joint understanding by management and labor as a "condition of employment." It cannot be something that one party just decided would be the best for the company or organization.
- *Longevity/Repetition:* There is no standard time frame as to how long a certain practice must exist or what frequency with which it must be realized in order to be considered a bona fide past practice. The more the practice repeats and with a greater length of time the more it is considered a past practice.[4]

## COACHES CORNER

Educational leaders are always dealing with labor in consideration of contracts, agreements, labor law, and the inevitable past practice. Many times, handshake deals are only used in the field to dictate some type of agreement onsite between an individual supervisor, principal, etc. and one of his team members and not something that would affect or make changes for multiple members of a faculty or organization.

An example of a handshake agreement may be someone leaving early for a doctor's appointment, or a quid pro quo that includes an extra assignment or task one day in exchange for a similar task on a different day.

The inevitable "past practice" term is something that will surface throughout the career of the executive in education and other industries, and he will have to work to negotiate carefully in order to generate a change that he needs as he navigates the actions and deeds of former executives. It is important to understand that past practice works both ways as well.

However, agreeing to negotiate through new terms to create an understanding that will help move the educational system forward is the most formidable course of action to take when faced with issues that the leader himself didn't create in the first place and has limited information on the history of said decisions.

Any executive should always strengthen his professional development in the area of contract interpretation and implementation when dealing with multiple units of workers and associations in the organization. Negotiating a contract and "getting it right" the first time will solve many potential disputes since an agreed upon process for negotiating the outcome concluded prior to when the actual outcome was reached. In other words, the issue was argued and solved before it ever really existed.

Now, at times, the contract needs to be interpreted differently due to a changing climate, the needs of a community, mandates, and the demands of students and families. That's where the daily negotiations come into play.

It is important for the education executive to fully understand that when the labor force wins, he wins as well. The farther outside the classroom or lecture hall the leader is, the more he needs the partnership and respect of those men and women who get up each and every day and settle into the "trenches." The only sure way to get there is to work together and agree on what is best for the system as a whole.

## YOU MAKE THE CALL: CASE SCENARIO

It has been several years since the office secretaries have negotiated a new contract at your district/organization. They have sat by while all other units have had their contracts evaluated and their salaries increased.

Elenora Dwyer is the most senior administrative assistant, and she has requested to have a meeting with you and the regional labor union representative to discuss some much-needed changes to the salary guide, workday, and vacation periods.

You meet with Elenora and Mr. Watt, the union shop steward. After you sit down, Mr. Watt starts the conversation with, "You know, it's been way too long that this group has had a raise or anything when everyone else has. Actually, I'm surprised that they had to reach out to you for this meeting."

What plays would you call?

The rest of the negotiation really depends on how you handle the comment and your own pride. What are some of the different approaches to a meeting that begins in such an interesting way?

What are your play calls to ensure that you "follow up" with this unit?

What do you do to enhance morale while you are considering changes or additions to the current agreement?

## NOTES

1. United Electrical, Radio & Machine Workers of America, 2021. "Winning Past Practice Grievances," https://www.ueunion.org/stwd_pastprac.html. Excerpted from Robert M. Schwartz, *How to Win Past Practice Grievances* (Cambridge, MA: Work Rights Press, 2001).

2. Amalgamated Transit Union, 2021. "Past Practice," https://www.atu.org/trainingvideos/billbarry-session4/Past-practice-grievances.pdf.

3. Ibid.

4. Ibid.

*Chapter 12*

# It's Not What You're Selling, It's How You're Selling It

Negotiation tactics and true influence include the way leadership navigates the importance of not only the actions needed for successful outcomes but how those actions are put forth to colleagues, subordinates, constituent groups, and other stakeholders.

Real focus must be put on the delivery, tact, and posture of any negotiated situation in order to ensure a specific and meaningful outcome for both sides. Specific to when leadership speaks with (not "to" or "at") labor leaders and individual employees, it is an absolute necessity that the school executive is grounded enough to understand that a smile goes a long, long way.

Negotiating to influence is no different than acting like a salesperson negotiating a sale. Data and evidence will benefit your position in any argument, but providing some give-and-take will solidify the leader's goal in getting what is needed in the end.

Let's be clear. Ensuring a noncombative atmosphere in any situation through "soft" tactics and maybe a "smile" must not be confused with being weak. On the contrary, using such tact to persuade and influence any type of decision or process with other units, team members, or employees can work in your favor while being the smartest and least stressful process to negotiating a win.

There does, however, come a time when the school executive or supervisor must posture, stand firm, and even become argumentative in order to get what she needs for her side of the organization. Although that may seem like a confrontational statement, at times just the effect that attaches itself to the heightened disagreement is more important than the need itself.

Take as an example parents who reprimand their children in order to correct their mistakes and provide a "teachable moment" when needed. If the parent yells and admonishes their child for every single instance, the "yelling" becomes just another Pavlovian result from a stimulus set forth by the child himself. The response becomes regular, and the effect is minimal to nonexistent.

Instead, if a parent only uses a harsh, verbal reprimand at the most opportune times, the effect is much greater and will cast a more memorable spotlight on the immediate situation. In other words, an individual should not elicit a greater frequency of responses unless he wants to saturate those responses with unimportant detail. The same holds very true for the school executive who is attempting to coax or make a point with her workforce.

As perception also must be a strong component and skill that is a major part of every school executive's playbook, the executive must also be extremely confident in herself and her ability to meet the needs of her stakeholders. At any given moment, she must "win over a room" and be prepared to ensure that her confidence is felt throughout all employees and supervisors in every department.

That overwhelming confidence—not cockiness—will help to define the daily mission of the organization while creating that sense of pride in the rest of the organization to be part of that desire for success. Workers and managers alike must be in awe of her, and that only stems from her ability to hold firm in the presence of adversity and ensure that any and all changes are met head-to-head with input from her teams outlining their needs and wants.

## COACHES CORNER

Educational leaders value good customer service—it is an absolute integral part of the job. Too often, executives have a difficult time finding the right way—no, the perfect way—to ensure that everyone in the school system or institution agrees with or understands the decisions that are being made or why they are taking place.

The bottom line is that any decision the educational leader makes is a decision that will lead to an outcome at some point. In other words, there is nothing in the executive's way to stop her from deciding what she can or cannot do in consideration of the workforce and the organization. The possible ramifications that may stem from the decision being made, well that's a different story.

What helps at times is how the decision is delivered to the team. Again, teachers, subordinates, staff members, and the like all know that the executive is "the boss," and she is going to make the call. Why shouldn't she? Every decision—good or bad—rests on her shoulders, and at every wrong turn, she may not be responsible but she definitely is to blame.

To help soften any negative outcome or outcry for the decision being made by the executive, the delivery of that decision to the team and the input from stakeholder groups must be "packaged" and presented in a way that shows she has the knowledge base and a concern for the community and the individuals who are directly related to the decision being made.

Involving labor leaders and other individual stakeholder groups in every possible decision, program, or policy that affects the district, school, college, or university is the most efficient way that the executive can insulate herself from taking full responsibility for something that just "doesn't work" since it will have traveled to the forefront by passing stakeholders and receiving pertinent data and insight to deliver the best-informed decision. Oh, and smiling doesn't hurt either!

## YOU MAKE THE CALL: CASE SCENARIO

Caleb Varner is one of your new employees who is eager to learn everything about his job and provide the most thorough planning objectives for his students. You have noticed that Caleb on several occasions has stayed late to finish plans or reports and return parent phone calls. At times, he is even staying later than you.

Your lead supervisor, Molly Slater, came into your office to tell you she overheard several employees in the lunchroom talking about how the "new guy" is making all of them look bad.

Molly explained that several employees had stayed late one evening and saw you speaking to and laughing with Caleb. One employee was overheard expressing that she was with the organization for eight years now, and she has barely even had a conversation with you.

> What plays would you use to address Caleb, Molly, and the other employees affected by the situation at hand?
> What are some future actions you can take to help repair and strengthen morale?

*Chapter 13*

# When to "Go to the Mattresses"

As the chapter title is coined from the prominent idiom from *The Godfather*[1] cinematic culture, the school executive must know when to posture and do "battle" at the most appropriate times to ensure positive outcomes and avert resistance. It is that sure sense of understanding adversity that prepares the school executive for knowing when to utilize plays from his playbook that will create chaos and disrupt the status quo.

Every executive leader who subscribes to wanting a successful career in any industry should become a serious student of *The Godfather* saga. Excluding the violence that accompanies the methods of the early twentieth-century men of the "underworld" throughout the trilogy, the lessons, metaphors, politics, and business-savvy decisions that occur within the scenes are indicative of the mantra and plight of a family that closely emulates a labor force working hard to produce and compete each and every day.

And even though whole semesters of courses have been scheduled in colleges and universities based just on the saga in and of itself, many of the most memorable lines and scenes from the trio deal with influence and production through relations with labor. When Clemenza, who is a Corleone caporegime, tells his driver Paulie (who is five minutes away from getting "whacked") that acting Don Sonny Corleone wants to "go to the mattresses," the metaphor is set to reflect a standoff and battle that will last so long that no one will be returning home for some time.

As this text has continued to reference, working out differences with employees and labor/union leaders benefits all areas of the organization. A school executive's ability to utilize her playbook to prevent issues from arising at inopportune times and to even solve disputes before they become out of control or even irreparable is favorable to the growth of any district, system, or organization.

An individual can take the easy way around any differences and give in to the demands of his workforce and their association. However, we then wouldn't call him a leader and he most likely would lose the title of "executive." True, many of the plays that are practiced and perfected deal with compromise and include ways to entice the other side to come to terms with some type of agreement. However, even if each and every play is perfectly executed, there will always be a time that the executive will decide to "go to the mattresses" and take the argument head-on in order to prove some point, effectuate a necessary change, end a practice, or posture for position.

As the decision to avoid compromise will always seem apparent, it's actually more important to know exactly "when" the fight will occur. Choose to enter the battle too soon and the executive will run the risk of losing much capital and several relationships. If she waits until after the disagreement settles down for a while, she will mostly lose the element of surprise and face her problem in the public spotlight.

When deciding to use this particular play, the executive must understand that the battle is to be fought at any cost and may cause losses on both ends. Remember, this is usually an option only after all other attempts have been exhausted.

The school executive making the decision to stand his ground and argue until exhaustion must use cues to determine the appropriate time to wage his influence. These cues are supported by several determining factors when making such an important decision.

### The issue has already caused too much damage for compromise.

Here, the executive has exhausted all efforts of compromise and negotiation, and he has already lost the respect of his colleagues, workers, and external influencers due to the situation at hand. Sometimes, the damage to capital is too far along to ever repair. This especially holds true when outside forces, usually not even part of the organization, or the individual issues that are being discussed get too involved and provide an intensified, dramatic awareness to the situation.

### The losses (political capital; monetary; etc.), prior to the start, are too high.

The school executive may need to initiate greater tactics to end the conflict if she has already lost or has increasingly diminished her political capital and/or budget due to the circumstances surrounding the conflict. Although monetary losses can always be recuperated through other opportunities or business partnerships, the loss of political capital based upon disagreements with others or the dissemination of rumors and rhetoric in and around the workplace can be detrimental to an executive's status in the company or organization and thwart her own ability to get certain parts of the job "done" and her goals successfully completed.

## The executive has already lost ground or support from his team.

When the school executive realizes that his immediate team is no longer fully in support of either him or his cause based on an external conflict or an unwillingness to compromise, the decision to stand his ground and battle for position must ultimately be made. At this point, not only will everyone know the position of the executive and the direction in which he is heading with regard to the issue, but the executive will be able to "flush out" those internal team members who are loyal as opposed to those members who may be wavering.

### COACHES CORNER

An outsider may think that since education deals with academics, learning, children, and parent groups that too often executives in the field are easily swayed or "give in" without a fight. Well, those individuals could be no farther from the truth.

Granted, a successful educational leader knows that dealing with issues timely and in conjunction with his workforce and labor leadership usually leads to the more beneficial outcome for the entire community involved. Since decisions involve the lifestyle and global preparedness for the future leaders of industries and companies around the world, it is advantageous for many stakeholders to be in agreement on the decisions made, programs created, and the professional development opportunities for everyone invested in the educational community.

When dealing with educational staff members and the labor force, there is always time to be nice ... until it's time not to be nice. There is only so much compromise and accommodation that can be made by the executive until a more forceful approach is needed. This may be in the form of a reprimand, suspension, or some other sanction that will not only provide some remediation for a problem that occurred but put the individual on notice that it cannot happen again.

The paramount act to consider is when the appropriate time is to raise awareness of the issue to such an elevated level. "Going to the mattresses" too early and unprepared can leave the executive vulnerable and on the losing end of a long, drawn-out battle with attorneys and labor leaders within the organization. Waiting too long to do battle may leave the executive far past the ability to win in consideration of the situation at hand, and put him in harm's way by losing control over that particular situation while weakening his position for future confrontations.

## YOU MAKE THE CALL: CASE SCENARIO

You and other members of your administrative council have been discussing and negotiating new second-shift hours for your custodial workers with your shop stewards and union representatives for the last three weeks.

Every time you feel like you are making progress at coming to a mutually beneficial decision for both the organization and the employees, it seems that another "need" arises and pushes the negotiations "off track." Each time a session is over, the shop stewards return to the employees to report that "nothing is budging. No one really cares about getting this done."

You are convinced that this is a tactic being used to boost support during the negotiation sessions and the beginning of establishing grounds for a work action in the near future.

It is the evening before the next negotiations meeting, and you receive an email from your secretary informing you that the union has to cancel negotiations due to "unforeseen circumstances." Disappointed, since you moved several personal plans around to accommodate the meeting, you express some concern that the meeting is canceled so late in the process but move forward.

After lunch the next day, your assistant walks into your office and explains that she just had lunch with some coworker friends who said that word is going around that you are refusing to meet with the union to continue negotiations, and you didn't even give a reason why you canceled the session. Your assistant, who knew the real story, was careful not to mention anything about the email, but she wanted to let you know.

Word is traveling fast about your deciding not to meet.

What plays do you call?
What is your follow-up to the committee with regard to the rumors you are hearing?

## NOTE

1. Francis Ford Coppola, dir., *The Godfather* (United States: Paramount Pictures, 1972).

## Chapter 14

# Communication Is Key

There are several different styles of communication that are appropriate to use in specific situations dealing with labor relations and negotiations with labor units. Specifically in workplace relationships, there are four basic styles of communication that can be utilized depending upon the outcome that a leader is seeking. Passive; aggressive; passive-aggressive; and assertive techniques are styles of communication utilized by leaders and management to ensure that communication remains consistent and regulated in a prescribed manner aligned with the needs of the leader and/or organization.

It is important to understand that although each of these styles of communication has specific and inclusive barriers and boundaries to help assist leaders in communicating terms with employees and labor association membership, true persuasive communication techniques inspire actions, engage all members of an audience, and help to ensure the appropriate and needed outcomes are realized.

### Passive

Taking a "back seat" when communicating can be seen as a strategy and/or tactic to provide an individual who the leader is communicating with an opportunity to express his needs and wants in advance of the leader sharing her position. This play may be beneficial in consideration of letting the other side make the first offer with regard to some type of compromise or the terms to an agreement.

### Aggressive

An aggressive style of communicating with employees and members of the labor force is a play that can be dangerous if not executed correctly. In negotiating terms or arguing a point of contention, an aggressive front may work when the executive needs to set a tone, establish some leverage, or needs to posture because she is upset or angry at what occurred.

Being aggressive must not cross the line into bullying, meaning that the school executive won't let the labor side interact during the discussion or lay out an explanation of the argument. Instead, the executive can only come out as wholly aggressive if he understands what the fallout may be if the situation lends itself to him being labeled as the protagonist, perpetuating the issue instead of attempting to mitigate it.

### Passive-Aggressive

The school executive who expresses negative feelings towards a situation or an action in lieu of being transparent and addressing those concerns in the open is exhibiting a passive-aggressive style of communication. If not controlled correctly, this play may hurt the executive greatly since his interactions may be seen as "fake" or placating others.

### Assertive

Although sometimes confusing, using an "assertive" play versus an "aggressive" play deals with a certain level of respect between the executive and the labor leadership. Being aggressive is most often seen as insulting or abusive while assertive is standing one's ground without backing down in a negotiation or standoff.

## COACHES CORNER

One of the most important things educators teach students is how to communicate effectively with others. Even in postsecondary education we find college classes designed with "communication" in the title, lending itself to the belief that this is an extremely important tool that an individual should possess in his own life. Good communication is essential in both personal and professional relationships as well as when engaged in conversation via media platforms and in electronic correspondence.

An educational leader, building executive, principal, supervisor, or other member of the administrative team must communicate his goals and the reasoning behind his actions to his staff and labor force in very clear and concise terms. Further, the message being communicated must be perceived as having been appropriately better by the administration in order for there to be strong support for getting to that final outcome.

Good communication between educational executives and labor leaders can only reach an appropriate and necessary level if there is a sense of full transparency from the executive. The easiest way for this to occur is for her to keep labor leaders "in the loop," and to reach out first and often when the need arises.

During periods of discussion or conflict between the administration and labor leadership, both the executive and the labor leader are considered on the same hierarchical rung of the organizational structure for the purpose of dealing with the conflict at hand. Some educational leaders have a difficult time understanding why this would be the case, and the communication turns flat, sporadic, or even nonexistent at times. These individuals can't seem to get past the power struggle and their own need to micromanage and dominate every single situation that occurs.

Instead, the executive should utilize this as an opportunity to share both the burden and the praise of the decisions made as the shared vision would indicate strong communication between both the managerial and labor sides of the organization. The perfect picture of working together would continue to move the educational system forward while growing respect for the executive and strengthening the relationship the executive has with the union leaders.

## YOU MAKE THE CALL: CASE SCENARIO

Marco Tico is a cafeteria worker in your organization, and he was hoping to discuss a job posting with you for his son, Fabio, who just graduated college. Marco has been with the district/system for more than twenty years, is a hard worker, and a loyal employee. You recall hearing some stories about his son while he was away at college, but that was several years ago.

There are no specific policies regarding the hiring of family members or spouses.

What plays do you call?
What are some of the underlying and apparent concerns and considerations for hiring employees in your organization, especially when those new individuals already have a connection to a member of your labor force?
How do you mitigate some of those concerns and ultimately make a decision?

## Chapter 15

# Trust

Trust is a major tenet of any relationship. Where leaders and managers work with employees to advance productivity, trust among each other becomes the most important commodity. A strong educational leader must explore and utilize methods to strengthen trust between both the management and labor sides of the organization and outline strategies that are useful to help repair relationships.

The school executive must strive to build the level of trust between her and her work force on a daily basis. Without this as the foundation of the working relationship, no other objective or mission can be accomplished. In fact, it is almost certain that a lack of trust in leadership will lead to the weakening and ultimate demise in the leadership of the executive and the organization as a whole.

## Building Trust

In his playbook, the school executive must utilize several key strategies in order to ensure that he continues to build trust among all of his employees spanning each and every department. This includes:

*Be Transparent*

The executive should be as transparent as possible when dealing with situations and expressing concerns with the district, organization, and its members. It must be understood and expected that not every report or announcement from the chief will always consist of "good news," or be accepted by stakeholders.

However, the executive cannot be faulted or blamed for keeping her teams informed, and that will raise the level of trust, especially if she shares the really poor news as well as the good news.

## Include Stakeholders in the Decision-Making Process

The school executive who involves her stakeholder groups in developing the process of and making decisions for the company will raise the level of trust her employees have in her just by virtue of her trusting their opinion in the first place.

Trust is a two-way street, and individuals in district or institution settings will be trustworthy and loyal appointees as long as they feel that they are trusted as well. The executive may not agree with all of the suggestions from her workers, but her ability and willingness to sit and listen to the ideas and concerns from her stakeholders will build trust throughout the entire group.

## Repairing Trust That Has Been Damaged

The school executive can control the narrative when the relationship with labor leaders or workers in the field has been damaged by reaching out to discuss his concerns as soon as they arise. Knowing that there was a trust concern and being able to fully identify and be willing to work at the root issue causing this disconnect is the first major step when attempting to repair the trust that is lost.

The executive who is truly willing to repair the damage must be prepared to make some concessions in order to ensure that the trust issues can be repaired in a timely manner. Don't misunderstand me—one does not have to acquiesce and accept responsibility for everything that has occurred. Rather, working out a plan of action that introduces the important decision to repair all trust issues in the company or organization will be beneficial to all parties and the organization as a whole.

## Trust Is a Two-Way Street

As I stated in the aforementioned section, trust is a two-way street. One entity cannot earn trust while the other side is doing what it can to hurt the relationship. Building trust takes constant monitoring and an absolute "buy-in" from every party involved. Certain moves and decisions by the executive will take the labor side "off guard," and it is important for everyone to understand that the reasoning behind the decisions is the best for the entire work community.

## The Fallout That Comes with Breaking Trust

The fallout that comes when trust is broken can be detrimental to the school executive and her relationship with the entire system or organization. The greater fallout is not the initial impact in consideration of the immediate issue, but the inability for the leader to be seen as trustworthy moving forward when other issues surface. The executive must do everything in her power to repair any issues prior to the fallout becoming too unmanageable.

## COACHES CORNER

If a parent can't trust the district, institution, or individuals in a particular school when she drops off her child in the morning, then nothing else seems to matter. For several decades, adults took for granted that all education systems were the safest places for their children to "live" eight hours each and every school day.

Included in that definition is the trust that parents and other community members place in the entire labor force to meet the needs of the adolescents in the town based on guidelines, policies, programs, and protocols that usually are some reactions to a political agenda, societal change, or pedagogical "idea" of an overachieving individual with a power play to make such a lasting impression. Our urgency to trust others compels our guard to be up in certain situations; however, that need has greatly intensified over some recent considerations relative to violence in our nation's educational spaces and the pandemic.

What is sometimes missing is the trust that educational leaders have in labor leaders and vice versa. The nature of the game is a "cat and mouse" type of relationship where one is always looking to "catch" the other in some unavoidable situation or quandary.

The cliché that trust is a two-way street will never grow old or irrelevant. One can only get trust if he gives trust. On many occasions, the labor and school leaders must work in tandem to accomplish what they have promised their constituent groups would be an appropriate outcome. With time, trusting one another becomes the only way to keep the important goals, established for the community, in the forefront to enhance learning.

Trusting one another becomes that essential play that the executive must practice in order to ensure it will provide a positive outcome when it is needed the most. Usually in education, it needs to be strongest during negotiations, times of tragedy, or at crucial moments when decisions are being made that affect the entire school community.

## YOU MAKE THE CALL: CASE SCENARIO

You have been the chief school executive of your organization for eleven years, and the board has just extended your contract and provided you with a healthy increase and benefits package. As a system, things are going great! Productivity and scores are the highest they have been in five years.

Several days after your contract extension was announced over social media and on local business news feeds, one of your trusted program directors (and a good friend) takes you out for a celebration dinner. During the appetizer course, he starts to tell you that one of your directors, Danielle Devereux, was seen with some individuals in an attempt to halt your contract extension with several of the newer members of the board. Although you were not surprised, you were unsure as to why Danielle would make such an attempt at your tenure as chief, in that she does not have the experience one would need to be successful in the role.

The next day, you confirm what you heard at dinner with some of the board members you are close to. As is the daily routine, Danielle comes by your office to engage in small talk and discuss a new program you and she had been designing together for some time.

> What plays do you call?
> What are your long-term and short-term goal scenarios for your professional relationship with Danielle?
> What is your next play specific to Danielle and the concerns you have with her failed coup?

*Chapter 16*

# Strong Leadership on Both Sides

The importance of strong leadership on the school executive and labor leader sides of an organization is essential to the strength, survival, and growth of the organization as a whole. The leadership values and tools that individuals must possess in order to lead an organization or business to success—in consideration of both management and the workforce—are critical to establishing a good rapport, enhanced morale, mental wellness, and stability in any industry.

The successful school executive must ensure that he strengthens his leadership skills by continuing his professional development and keeping current and in-tune with the newest theories, laws, programs, and regulations pertinent to his employees and the mission of the organization itself. Without advancing and "sharpening" his leadership skills, the executive will be unable to raise his teams and workforce to the next goal, or worse—fail in assisting his employees in recovering from missed attempts at meeting benchmarks or feeling success at the workplace.

Although most school executives would rather an individual workforce leader or representative be less powerful and less efficient than she is, it can be argued that strong leadership on both "sides" leads to a greater sense of checks and balances, which then leads to stronger accountability, innovative creativity, and increased production overall. With the end goals in sight, the issues arise when one considers what occurs in the daily interactions between both leaders. The school executive's playbook then must be filled with tactics, considerations, and formulated actions that allow both sides to value a "give-and-take" type of relationship where all constituent groups can respect the role of the executive and the leader on the labor side of the workforce.

As an executive has her administrative team or cabinet to help manage the day-to-day tasks and operations of the educational organization, the employee side can be represented by formal means (labor union) or an informal structured balance (informally "elected" coworkers who act as liaison to management). It is also probable that the executive may work directly with employees independently who are not part of any local association or representation but possibly a national association or representative body (e.g., exempt employees working in the school business office).

Regardless of formal or informal means of representation, one thing is certainly clear: both sides must place a high value on working conditions and morale while providing refined definitions of what is expected of both the management and labor components of the organization. This can only be done through the clear communication of the goals set for both the organization and the employees, both collectively and as individuals.

For example, a school district employs 3,500 teachers and staff members to run its twenty-six neighborhood schools. The chief education officer and the board establish a mission and vision statement that directly outlines the overarching goals for the students in the city, each specific school building population, and each school faculty as well.

As the aforementioned scenario deals with the communication of goals set forth collectively for the group, each teacher or employee also has his/her own professional goal as well. This now ensures that leadership maintains an active role in the oversight of action plans that lead to the advancement of individual goals, that then lead to the attainment of building goals, that, in turn, will lead to the successful realization of the mission.

Here is another scenario based on the same example. A collective bargaining agreement is established for all members of the faculty and staff by the local union. Regardless of the individual's intent to join the association or not, the agreement and its parameters hold true for all faculty and staff throughout the district. Within this agreement, each individual has his/her own separate salary based on years of service, degree, and several other factors based on the individual's time on task and professional development. Thus, it is in each individual's best interest to ensure that he/she surpasses the standards as established by the leadership of both sides.

As there are different forms of leadership style for each individual leader, the executive's strength lies in her ability to create a strong team by leveraging the attributes and strengths from the labor leadership. This can be in the form of teaming, negotiating style, or just an overall ability to formulate alliances with factions of the workforce that are burdensome to the executive.

In all, the ability to lead all areas of the organization must be established early in any relationship and through the continued realization that the work must be accomplished together for ultimate success. Remember, the grievances and disagreements should be all business—never personal. With the mission always in sight to exemplify pride in the entire company or organization, one thing is certain. A mutual respect should exist between leaders from both sides.

## COACHES CORNER

An educational system thrives when leadership on the administrative and labor sides is very strong and dedicated to a shared mission for the district, school system, or institution. When leaders come together and support a shared vision, there is a heightened respect and level of dedicated support from all stakeholder groups in consideration of the tasks that need to be completed to meet the goals as established through cooperative measures.

As this leadership resonates throughout the system, nearly all areas will see growth since there is a true direction and road map to work through any issue or roadblock that the teams may come across during their progression. This strong command of the needs and vision of the system will "trickle-down" to other members of the organization ensuring that the tenets of strong leadership are apparent in all areas of the organization.

To be fair, at times strong leadership on both the administrative and labor sides of the table can lead to posturing and a push for leverage in order to persuade a position one way or the other. In the process, things may get delayed and the true reason for the decision may get lost in all of the discussions. In spite of this, strong leadership will be able to work through those considerations and come together for what is best for the educational value and the climate of the district or organization. Strong leaders create positive actions that are contagious—this is the easiest way to ensure all of the needs of the system are met.

## YOU MAKE THE CALL: CASE SCENARIO

Your supervisor of facilities, Henry Fadala, has just announced that he is "grooming" his assistant, Mia Landau, to take his position after he retires in a few years. It is no secret that more can get accomplished in consideration of management-labor issues with Mia making all of the decisions.

A major order for a shipment of supplies was just secured by the maintenance team, and the district/organization will need to increase shift work throughout the nighttime to ensure delivery expectations to the school sites are met before the holiday closure.

Your initial discussions with Henry about workflow and other labor necessities causes Henry to take pause and be reminded of similar projects that were unsuccessful many years prior to your arrival at the organization.

In fact, Henry has gone so far as to insist that he may need to contact union counsel from the national office to help with discussions and other items that need to be negotiated. You are not against working with labor leadership and representatives to discuss additional time and compensation based on increased workload and expectancy; however, as the contract depends on a time "crunch," involving members outside the local arena who don't have any personal "skin in the game" will only delay work efforts and diminish timelines.

Mia has intimated that workers are willing to get started, and they would really enjoy this opportunity to make some additional money just prior to the holiday.

What plays do you call?
What are some, if any, legal, ethical, and moral considerations you should contemplate prior to making any additional moves forward?
How do you work to ensure Mia is taking more of a supervisory role during the transition?

*Chapter 17*

# The Willingness to Make Concessions

The school executive doesn't always have to be in active contract negotiations with her workforce to need the knowledge base and negotiation skill to compromise on a nearly daily basis. The executive should include in her playbook several ways to ensure that there is always a Plan B (and a Plan C) as well as items or attenuations to policies and procedures that she can use to assist her when negotiating an action with her employees and team members.

There must be a give-and-take relationship where leadership learns to include concessions in successful negotiations in order to acquire what is necessary for progress. There are several steps to ensuring this occurs in order to continue to strengthen the relationship between the executive and her teams and grow the respect for labor leadership that is necessary for future compromises:

**Identify which concessions can be made/afforded.**

A leader must enter the conflict or negotiation knowing which concessions can be made, at what cost, and how many. This is an important part of understanding what impact you can make during any type of compromise or session with an employee or association.

**Anticipate the impact that will occur on both sides when the concession is agreed to.**

Understanding the impact seems like an "of course I will" statement, but far too many negotiations occur with executives unprepared to give something to get something. This mostly concerns knowing how to prepare oneself for a meeting of this importance; however, one can only be prepared by trying to understand and then anticipate the "plays" of an adversary. With this information ready prior to any decisions on compromise, the play falls into the executive's possession, and the impact is minimized since it has already been calculated and accounted for.

**Ensure that the final concession will ultimately solve the compromise needed.**

After meeting and negotiating a compromise (or two), it is crucial that the executive assures that no other compromise or change will take place after the agreement is finalized. Without said assurance, future negotiation sessions for contract or work-related considerations will not be valued in a reputable manner. This holds true for both the management and labor sides. When both sides agree to "leave the table in compromise," they decide right at that point that each side is satisfied, progress was made, and the relationship is stronger because both sides learned to work together for a common goal.

It is also important to ensure that the workforce is informed that the executive and the employees/labor leadership have worked tirelessly to ensure that a compromise led to better conditions, and that the entire team values the continued success of the school system, institution, or organization.

## COACHES CORNER

In education, individual facilitators teach, breathe, and live in a world where compromise is necessary in order to engage learners and elevate their comprehension to the next level. Making concessions in order to ensure equity in access for different groups of learners and stakeholder bands has become second nature in consideration of the need for social awareness and enhanced wellness for all members of the community.

Administrators and executives must be willing to make concessions in order to ensure that faculty, staff, and students feel that their needs are being met and their concerns are being considered. Further, it is "OK" for the administrator to feel that she is giving more than she is getting. Understandably, productivity must be taking place. But it isn't always a negative outlook if an executive or supervisor has to make multiple concessions for an individual who is truly struggling with a concept, initiative, or something else that may be affected by his personal life.

This is not to be mistaken for assisting someone in the classroom or on the supervisory team who may be taking advantage of what the executive is doing. Once vetted, the leader will be able to evaluate why the individual is struggling and then continue to assist him in getting through the issue, or not. In time, the executive's willingness to make concessions will be reviewed and her attention given to assist through compromise will be duly noted.

Here, the leader gains the respect of her constituents by being seen as patient and understanding while not giving up hope on someone who is having a difficult time. This is the same type of care and concern the leader must expect from her employees when they interact with students, other employees, parents, and the community.

## YOU MAKE THE CALL: CASE SCENARIO

Making concessions to ensure productivity and positive morale can help a school, district, institution, college, or university progress.

Think about your own current (or past) institution or organization. What are some concessions you can give if you were to look to make a compromise for the following conflicts?

- More overtime/extra-pay duties that rotate equally among workforce members.
- Merging two job descriptions into one new position.

How would you present these concessions to stakeholder groups or labor leaders?

*Chapter 18*

# The Art of Negotiation

Terms are negotiated for almost every decision made in consideration of the daily operations of any organization or business. The same holds true in educational systems, school districts, and institutions of higher learning throughout the world. Negotiations can occur formally in long, distinct sessions to discuss changes and additions to collectively bargained contracts, to individual one-to-one compromise with the labor force at the organization to discuss conditions and future considerations for events that occur during day-to-day operations.

The art of negotiation includes an intricate system of strategies and tactics useful for leaders in nearly all decision-making instances, especially where contract negotiations are considered. This text does not attempt to discuss those negotiation schemes that should be incorporated in an executive's playbook as useful plays to execute when the need arises.

Rather, this space is utilized as a marker to encourage you to find time to study negotiation, as it is an art form, and to make one thing clear—successful negotiation is the ultimate key to ensuring growth for the company and an executive's professional career path.

Without the ability or knowledge to negotiate terms and leverage any and all types of individual and collective occurrences in the workplace, the leadership and mission is seen as one-sided, and animosity, regret, and disloyalty start to play an active role in forming the landscape of the workplace. Although there is an appropriate time when an absolute directive must be given and then followed in its pure entirety, not many individuals find excitement and satisfaction in performing what is dictated to them unless they are aware that there is some say or form of relief for them prior to, during, and/ or after the directive occurs.

The ability and need to negotiate many different areas of the workday and overall working environment must be an important goal for the school executive to work towards with each and every new day and interaction. As she negotiates effectively while navigating her employees and members on her leadership team, she strengthens her ability to get things accomplished that will help push the needle forward in consideration of nearly every aspect of the organization.

In her cycle of negotiations, it is critical that the school executive uses her plays, tactics, and negotiation style to preserve what she needs to get accomplished from the session while staying ahead of what the "other side" needs to gain in order to satisfy their constituent base. To be clear, the executive doesn't need to recognize what they "want" but should concentrate on what they feel they "need."

Following her training, professional development, and sorting through all of her experiences with past negotiations, the executive's playbook is filled with a knowledge base to deal with daily compromises and long-term collective agreements to persuade a successful incorporation of the needs of the employee with the allowable provisions of the system, institution, or organization.

## COACHES CORNER

This chapter discusses the art of negotiation in two considerations. First, negotiations between school executives and labor leaders in consideration of contracts, policies, and other tangible items that necessitate a true "back-and-forth" where both sides agree on terms and conditions for the workplace. In education, this includes boards of education, trustees, and attorneys working alongside executives and labor leaders to make changes to pay scales, time on task, and other protocols that occur on a daily basis.

Second, the art of negotiation is used more frequently in quick discussions that concern daily operations relative to the educational system and its employees, students, professors/teachers, and all other stakeholder groups. Educational systems constantly include negotiating compromise for nearly every foundational aspect of the education system. From cafeteria menus to teacher coverages, to grading policies, "curving," and instructors being consistent on providing make-up time for students in consideration of tests and work, the landscape of education includes a fabric of negotiating for survival and success.

When dealing with union leaders in academic settings, negotiations tend to be slow at times since many of the issues and concerns deal with personnel and students within specific time frames. This includes a shortened fiscal year, semesters, regulations dealing with FERPA and other considerations, and the overall size of the association or membership. As communication continues to be key between the leaders of both the management and labor teams, negotiating terms to meet both short- and long-term plans of action is the only way to continue to move the educational system forward.

Successful negotiations to enhance both systematic needs and the needs of the individuals involved throughout the educational organization only lends itself to greater advancement of the programs and metrics as established through strategic planning and an assessment of the needs of the system. The educational leader must remember that it is a negotiation, and both sides will struggle to find some common ground in order to ensure both sides feel that compromise was made. This will help to strengthen morale and lead to a more positive climate that will grow more successes for learners and leaders alike.

## YOU MAKE THE CALL: CASE SCENARIO

Jeremy Sinclair is one of the top dean candidates you are recruiting for your San Francisco office. Jeremy has narrowed his choice to both your institution and a competitor on the East Coast located only thirty-five minutes from his current home. Jeremy is willing to relocate and begin a new life if he can "find a place that is a perfect fit."

Jeremy will really make an impact on the programs at your institution.

What plays would you use?

Discuss several of the negotiation tools, alternate offers, and incentive packages that you could negotiate to entice Jeremy in joining your team.

How does negotiating a contract that may be broader in scope and include a greater benefit package than those of some of your current and long-standing employees impact the workplace in consideration of morale and productivity?

What plays can you use in anticipation of explaining such differences to your current staff members?

*Chapter 19*

# Response to Actions

At times, labor leadership and organized unions perform actions against management to stall production or provide negative publicity to make a point of concern known or thwart production in an attempt to persuade negotiations or enhance working conditions. Each of these types of actions serves a specific purpose and elicits specific leadership responses that are lawful and effective to ending the action.

Every school executive must know how to execute her plays in order to ensure a quick and efficient end to any work action that is initiated in an educational setting. This includes strong transparency, communication with stakeholders, and the ability to identify and negotiate a best alternate offer.

The school executive must also fully understand that her actions may ultimately cause reactions that could negatively impact her and her organization. In turn, any delays in communicating a compromise or reaching some type of agreement in consideration of a dispute with a contract, working conditions, or other perceived violation could likely cause a job action to "encourage" a change in philosophy, procedure, or protocols within the organization.

Further, actions bring an awareness to an otherwise private labor matter that could gain notoriety and attract differences of opinion while garnering support and a sympathetic "ear" from outsiders. This may then put pressure on the executive and the management team to take a closer look at the demands and accusations, causing a greater sense of urgency to assist in ending the conflict and any negative press.

Although it is not possible to always work through issues prior to a work/job action being implemented, a successful executive knows that his playbook is filled with ways to stall or sidestep the conflict altogether. However, when the play doesn't work well enough to halt the momentum of the workforce, it is imperative that the executive knows which work actions can cause the most issues when dealing with value and productivity.

## Strike

One can argue that this is defined as an action, but it is (or at least, should be) the last possible step when attempting to mitigate the situation between leadership and labor in any company or organization. Section 7 of the National Labor Relations Act states in part, "Employees shall have the right . . . to engage in other concerted activities for the purpose of collective bargaining or other mutual aid or protection" (National Labor Relations Board). This includes the right to "strike" with limitations based on the reasoning behind the walkout as defined by the Act.

Most of these actions fall into two categories: economic (wages, benefits, conditions) and unfair labor practice (issues with management, hiring/firing). The majority of states have statutorily made it illegal for state and public governmental employees to strike. This includes police and fire, teachers, and state officials in service positions that operate functions of government.

The earliest recorded strike in the United States occurred in 1768 when New York journeymen tailors protested a wage reduction. A strike halts production and services in an industry, and it is a terminal tactic used to attempt to reach a compromise, meet demands, or open lines of communication which have been closed due to dispute or disdain.

At times, a strike is viewed as an attempt to hurt or admonish the leadership or management of a company, organization, or a whole industry. The amount of damage a full work stoppage can cause not only affects the company itself (loss of profit), but the workers (loss of wages) and the consumers (price increases to cover lost costs) are also affected due to the decrease in productivity.

A tactic of this magnitude almost always defines a deadlock or impasse between management and labor. The posturing on both sides is so pronounced that communication is blurred or nonexistent, and once "idle" threats must be fulfilled to maintain control and possibly regain the upper hand in negotiation strategy.

Most strikes include public picketing where employees walk outside of a facility to protest. This causes a heightened public interest and may bring scrutiny to the company, organization, or an individual employer. In a time when social media is a rampant method of gaining immediate and global access to any and all social issues, public displays of turmoil and dissent are something that a chief executive must get a handle on in an immediate way.

Unfortunately, some protests from striking members of unions become emotionally charged and violence occurs. This is not the intended manner for the work action; however, the violence hurts the cause for both management and labor sides of the leadership teams. At all costs, strikes should be avoided, and it is the executive's duty to work with labor leadership to ensure the safety of workers and other constituent groups while compromise is being reached. It is important to remember that at some point, everyone will join together again as one team for the betterment of the company or organization.

## Work-to-Rule

Ultimately, a work-to-rule action is where employees do the bare minimum of their job description in order to meet the job requirements. This is often a first attempt at job action to get the attention of leadership and bring public awareness to an issue or problem. An example of a career industry who uses this action is teachers.

As educators in school settings usually utilize parameters outside a workday schedule to return parent phone calls, assist students, and volunteer to chaperone events, a work-to-rule action would find faculty and staff members completing only what is required of them during their prescribed work hours. This action gives an awareness to the "extra" work that the workforce performs on a daily basis without recognition or compensation.

## Intermittent Strike

Also known as a "slowdown strike" or a "go-slow," this is an illegal work action where the company's workforce fails to perform the job duties that the employer has previously and consistently required them to perform. These are job actions that involve the constant repetition of short strikes used by workers to pressure the executive to agree to the demands requested all while still receiving full wages for working.

## Overtime Ban

To an executive or manager, this work action seems "silly" while acting as the poster child for "don't bite off your nose to spite your face." On the surface, an overtime ban would seem to only hurt workers since they would be refusing extra pay.

On the contrary, this action is most detrimental to management since the afforded overtime is originally posted for some reason of production. In other words, overtime isn't just given to employees because the executive and her team want to "give" workers more money to make them feel good. Rather, overtime is covering an absence of labor, increased need for more production, or a specified job duty outside the contractual work day. A work action that bans the acceptance of overtime can be devastating.

### Blue Flu

Although this term was coined pursuant to the "call out" using sick leave of mass numbers of police officers, Blue Flu is an action that is utilized across every industry (sick out). The executive's playbook includes "plays" to help dissuade such actions through contract parameters including requests for medical notes to return to work.

Further, sick days are only permitted to be utilized when an employee is "ill," and these days are given to ensure an individual recuperates fully. In a time where social media is so prevalent, some employees who use sick time for personal reasons will inevitably make a post or share a location that negates their need to stay away from work due to illness.

### Sit-Down

An action where employees block entrances and "sit down" in protest, essentially taking possession of a business, property, or area. This action is illegal.

### Historical Work Actions

Work actions in the form of strikes occur globally on a daily basis. Some last minutes and others, days, weeks, or even months. Although it is impossible to create a recorded account of all of the actions that have occurred over time, it is important to study those most notable events so as to establish a pattern of labor tactics and explore the reasoning as to why these conflicts occur in the first place.

As an example, major league sports in America have had several lockouts and work actions that have led to changes in collective bargaining contracts, salary "caps," and league minimums. It is interesting to see that as one league follows through on an action, the other leagues aren't far behind.

Historical strikes are also relative to the social climate at the time. During the 1960s and '70s, actions included organic means, transportation, and other societal activism that was occurring around the nation. Further, patterns of actions that follow one another in transportation industries and raw materials are also interesting to analyze in consideration of price changes and global import and export issues during the same time frame as the work actions being recorded.

## COACHES CORNER

The best way to give a "pep" talk to leaders in administration when discussing giving responses to actions is to start with a quote from *The Prince*:[1]

> Any man who tries to be good all the time is bound to come to ruin among the great number who are not good. Hence a prince who wants to keep his authority must learn how not to be good, and use that knowledge, or refrain from using it, as necessity requires.

To many outside industry leaders, education executives do not come across as individuals who master an ability to know when and how to respond to harsh, threatening, or combative actions from adversaries. Such a Machiavellian maneuver as knowing when to react seems opposite of the tenets that educational systems attempt to instill in its most cherished commodity.

However, it can absolutely be argued that an important expertise of a very strong education executive is the very fact that he does know exactly when the appropriate time and venue is to respond to the actions of his labor leader and employees.

In an educational environment, some of the actions of the labor force when responding to something that has been implemented or implied by management are very limited. The nature of educating the youth of the nation bears with it the burden of being at work to provide compulsory education to all learners—each and every school day. Some of the actions can be adverse and nuanced enough with negativity to create animus toward the administration and Trustees through subtle actions that bring to light that there is a disconnect or disagreement between management and labor.

At times, adverse actions are detrimental to the progress of the educational system, and the longer the action the harder it is to repair the relationship. Thus, the executive needs to ensure his timing is right, knowing when to act accordingly to a response that has occurred.

## YOU MAKE THE CALL: CASE SCENARIO

You are working on a construction project at one of your buildings to expand a program area to host a new STEM lab. One of the subcontractors that your construction manager has decided to utilize employs workers that are not from any local union shop. You are made aware that the general contractor from RU Thayer Construction, LLC. (the approved lowest bidder) is upset that your manager has hired nonunion employees to oversee the worksite and manage the project for your organization.

On Monday morning, you drive by the site early to check on the progress that the crews are making, since the weather last week wasn't cooperating with the schedule that was first decided upon when the project began.

As you pull up to the site, you notice a large object on the side of the work area just next to the construction fence and in front of your school sign. Several early morning joggers have stopped to inquire about the object, taking selfies by it and laughing with each other.

Closer inspection reveals a large, twenty-foot blow-up rat anchoring the building. At its base are several union members holding signs that announce union labor is absent from the job. You also learn that several of your own maintenance crew and union members are deciding whether or not to "cross the line."

What plays do you use?
How do you communicate effectively with all parties?
What outside influencers may you need to consider in your conversations?
How do you inform stakeholder groups?

## NOTE

1. Niccolò Machiavelli, *The Prince* (Harmondsworth; New York: Penguin Books, 1981).

*Chapter 20*

# Anti-union Animus

At times, management's actions against labor can be considered unfair, unlawful, or egregious. There is a certain tone and dialogue a leader can utilize or avoid during certain controversial situations to help strengthen relations with union and labor leadership as well as strategies to ensure that management's position is considered in a serious manner.

Sometimes, the tone and demeanor of the school executive and his team may come across terse and disruptive, leaving the labor or workplace employees feeling intimidated, humiliated, or disrespected. Further, decisions can be perceived as going against a collective agreement, more specifically when union labor contracts are in place. The union leadership may also feel that decisions are made based on relationships between the chief executive and the union leader and even retaliatory if based on a response or interaction that comes directly after a union complaint or work action.

More specifically, an interaction or an employment decision made by the school executive or an administrator that is taken without a legitimate business motive and discriminates against another employee because of union activity is an action that is considered anti-union animus in nature. Although this is definitely something that occurs at times in response to a decision, statement, or action by a union labor leader, it is also very easy for the employee or labor leader to claim this type of discrimination based on the fact that he doesn't like what the executive said or the actions he took with regard to the incident or infraction.

Here, the school executive must tread carefully, and gain a strong sense for the tone of the conversation and the demeanor of the labor leader ensuring that the executive remains in control of the situation at hand. If the executive suspects that the conversation or action has reached such a level that the labor side will be defining the statement or action as anti-union animus, then the executive must immediately make sure he states his true intention for the statement or action, and to reiterate it is—in no way—retaliatory in nature. This should be followed with a written correspondence outlining what had occurred, the reason it had occurred, and that the executive immediately clarified the apparent misunderstanding.

On the other hand, there may come a time in the school executive's career where she has also perceived that she was treated unfairly, and she may decide that being outspoken, abrupt, and admonishing of some persons or ideology from the labor side is the best way to get a point across, "push back," and respond to an action that is intended to hurt her credibility with her team and staff.

Again, this may not seem like the best play on the surface; however, at times it is imperative that the executive shows that her willingness to compromise, negotiate, make concessions, and the like, shouldn't be viewed as being synonymous with weak. Although these types of actions against labor forces can lead to an unfair labor practice (ULP), at times the end seems to justify the means.

## COACHES CORNER

The actions of an educational leader who is perceived as going against an organized right of her labor association or union can be seen as having anti-union animus. These actions can include anything from trying to prevent the union itself from organizing (stopping employees from joining) to attempting to show a union leader as weak, lying, or as an inept representative of his people.

Regardless of the unfair labor practice that the executive is being charged with, it is a call for concern in districts, universities, and other educational areas that recognize unions as a part of the educational landscape. Sometimes anti-union animus is considered discriminatory against the labor association due to the fact that the action taken by the executive or educational leader is not relevant to the business operations of the school, district, or education system.

One common complaint that causes leaders to take pause in consideration of what is or is not unfair is when the executive involves himself in the everyday happenings of the union itself. This could include operations such as officer elections, sponsorships, political actions, and disputes against members.

Although some of the issues that unions and labor units seem to encounter closely bestride the line that separates union and district matters, it is very important for the executive to take a step back and observe the root cause of the problem to determine if it affects the district and its students as a whole or if it truly is a matter that relates to union business. Should the litmus test meet the standard for the latter, he must stay away from the conflicts that are occurring, even though he may have the urge to help mediate concerns or offer assistance.

## YOU MAKE THE CALL: CASE SCENARIO

You met early one day with your leadership team and division supervisors to discuss personnel changes and possible layoffs. It has also become apparent to your team that due to budget constraints and the need to downsize due to lowered enrollment, several members in the room would also be terminated at some point over the next several weeks.

Several supervisors are suggesting not to follow some of the policies and procedures that were put in place to protect employees from egregious hiring and firing practices as described in the collective bargaining agreement.

It seems that you are losing control over the meeting and its objective.

What play do you call?
How do you steer the leadership team back on task to the objective of keeping a productive workforce?

*Chapter 21*

# Pyrrhic Victories and Strategies of Labor Unions

Being successful after a challenge ensues only occurs when one understands and becomes a student of opposing strategies. Many times, leaders look to "win" single-point arguments while losing sight of the ultimate goal or mission. Leaders must consider all outcomes and have a true understanding that, at times, there must be compromise to mitigate loss and gainfully enjoy what has been acquired in a positive manner.

Let's face it—no one wants to lose! Power, influence, and positioning in an organization is a dog-eat-dog game that includes stepping on some "toes" and having people upset at times while inevitably climbing that proverbial ladder. However, a truly successful school executive can navigate each "battlefield" effectively and know when to retreat and when to even lose (gracefully) at times.

**Know what you can give up before you negotiate terms.**

Before negotiating or compromising the day-to-day decisions that need to be considered in the workplace, the school executive must fully take inventory on what she "has" to lose, give, and/or pass on prior to the conversations taking place. If the executive doesn't know what is in her arsenal that she can leverage in any short- or long-term negotiation sequence, then she will not have the ability or support to move forward with how she needs to compromise.

**Always look for two gets for every give.**

When negotiating to win, it is important to apply the rule of "two gets for every give." This will give the school executive a second pathway to attaining her goal, and it helps to establish a good negotiation pattern with her workforce. Further, asking for expanded terms on any item she is looking to compromise makes it easier to claim a victory and grow her value with her employees. Bottom line . . . two wins are always better than one!

**Work harder than the labor team.**

If he wants to win, the school executive must "want it more" and work harder than any member of the workforce at negotiating the items, working conditions, or concerns at hand.

**Lead by example.**

The school executive must lead by her own example, and she must consistently put theory into practice in order to strengthen her bond with her staff and enhance her role. Too often, leaders "talk the talk," but individuals must "show" their knowledge base and lead teams to success from the head of the line.

**Know that you are only successful if labor is successful.**

Pyrrhic victories provide school leaders with small triumphs at the sake of possibly losing in the long run. However, frequently the battles won come at a perfect time for the school executive to make a point that needs to be made. Also, "sharing" victories with the workforce and labor leaders allows both sides to feel empowered to strengthen the system or organization as a whole.

## COACHES CORNER

The educational landscape with its peaks and valleys of political terrain and personnel differences is the perfect backdrop for studying Pyrrhic victories. More often than not, compromise occurs between leaders and the labor force each day which outlines the structure of give-and-take among all areas of the organization.

Compromising some to gain much more is a mantra that executives live by across many industries. In education, this holds true with personnel decisions that are based on the needs of both the employee and the student. Something as simple as accommodating a teacher who needs to leave a few minutes early to pick up her sick father can yield much larger dividends in the future when the leader needs assistance or a volunteer or just someone to say, "hey, he's a nice guy" about him in the faculty room during a very bad day.

So where does a Pyrrhic victory fit in with education, labor, and strategy? At times, an executive or board must make some difficult decisions in order to ensure that a particular outcome occurs or a protocol is obtained. This decision may come at a greater cost to the system, but the "victory" holds more importance where it makes a significant contribution to upholding obligations in a contractual agreement, policy, or perceived protocols as set forth by leadership.

For example, a school administrator finds that several employees have been leaving early and not completing their work while other individuals had to cover for them in their absence. Although this could easily be settled with a reprimand, the executive felt that what occurred was so egregious and unfair to the other workers that she requested a withholding of increment for the individuals leaving early. The union challenged the executive, stating that these individuals never had any disciplinary actions prior to the current issue.

Here, the actions of the executive will lead to a Pyrrhic victory where the amount of money and time spent to challenge this disciplinary action will more than likely surpass what the actual outcome will be. An increment withholding of a salary could be less than $1,000; however, legal fees associated with fighting to uphold such an action can cost ten times as much.

Although this may seem to some as a waste of resources, to the executive the tone it sets for the other staff members and the support she will gain and experience from the remaining employees may seem silent but will exponentially grow the respect they feel for her. Hence, sometimes an executive must lose a battle at major costs to win the war.

## YOU MAKE THE CALL: CASE SCENARIO

Hank Spotswood and you have worked as labor leader and school executive for the last twelve years, helping to grow the educational system's accolades to national status. Most recently, you and Hank have been disputing the notion that a national holiday, which falls on a weekend, should be celebrated the following Monday and vacation time should be granted to all employees.

Although Hank doesn't know it yet, this is something that you are currently negotiating with the supervisors in their upcoming contract. Obviously, if you were to accept these terms with management but expect the labor force to report to work, a greater issue (or two) would arise.

What play do you call?

## Chapter 21

As was stated earlier, it may be more beneficial at times to lose a battle to win the entire war. If you choose to concede to Hank's request, what are some counteroffers that can be considered?

*Chapter 22*

# Avoiding Work Actions

Communication and compromise are two key skills that are necessary for school executives and administrators to utilize in order to avoid any possible negative labor reactions or work-related job actions that look to halt production and weaken the labor-management relationship. This is definitely one aspect of working with labor associations that should be avoided at all costs. This is not so much for the purposes of leverage, but rather it weakens the relationship between executives and labor through unnecessary means.

It is important first to define what a true work (job) action is versus a labor "strike." A work action is a temporary action (such as a slowdown) by workers as a protest and means of forcing compliance with demands for the management of an organization. It is not a direct stoppage of work production like a strike would be; rather, it is the minimal production effort afforded by the labor unit in order to grab the attention of leadership and—even, moreover—other interested parties who may force influence over the organization in labor's favor.

These actions vary from industry to industry, and they can include manual forces (an actual slowdown of production by the numbers) and other more subtle consequential reminders (the workforce all reports to work exactly at starting time) that ultimately affect output but still meet current contractual obligations. A work/job action is usually the first indication that "talks" between executive leadership and labor over contract, safety, and other workplace items have reached a "stall" and the immediate future does not include any continuation of having conversations with the hope of reaching some type of agreement or compromise.

A good union/labor leader will only orchestrate a work action when absolutely necessary. It is important for the school executive to understand why this is an important tactic for the "other" side.

First, regardless of how efficient the communication pipeline is on the labor side, a campaign that is established for a work action to be run successfully takes time and a large organized effort. This initially starts with a plan of action in which all members must agree. With any team, this is difficult. Any disagreement or different perspective on both the issue at hand and the action itself could be detrimental to the cause.

Next, not all employees may agree with the action. Yes, there will initially be "excitement" over the charge to come together and dispute the executive's actions, but getting everyone on board is extremely rare.

Finally, a union leader who sets a job action in place always runs the risk of having the school executive and his leadership team "outrun" the action itself. In other words, a job action that lasts days, weeks, or months with no movement to reference on the labor side would be seen as a failure and could inevitably weaken the labor leader's position of power. A good school executive knows that continuing to work through issues during a work action and extending the timeline can result in a weakening of the foundation for the issue that is being presented.

So, with the possible negatives attached for any union leader who puts an action in place, why would the school executive not want to take her chances and press the envelope? The simple answer is that creating chaos and bringing attention to an institutional problem instead of focusing all energy on the actual organization or the service provided to students is just bad business. Also, what we know about any and every issue (especially in the days of social media, cameras, etc.) is that there are always others who want to become a part of the issue.

In other words, instead of working out specific issues between the administration and labor, a work action brings attention to outside forces that may use the issue for publicity for their own personal agenda. It is very easy for a group (either local or national) to visit an issue, exponentially increase the awareness of that issue, and then leave.

What this does is put a greater spotlight on the problem at hand for the school executive, and that problem is usually one-sided. It is very difficult for an executive, who just received an incredible bonus for productivity from his employees, to argue that his employees don't deserve another raise. Or how about telling all of those elementary teachers, who are working after hours to help children become the future leaders of America, that their time and effort isn't worth a cost-of-living increase?

Thus, avoiding any type of work action is beneficial for the school executive on many levels. Some of these may be more personal than the next. The playbook for resolving such actions includes a strict regimen for every leader to consider when faced with this type of potential crisis.

## COACHES TIPS

**The school executive himself must be absolutely involved in the negotiating and compromise of the root cause of the action.**

It is imperative that the executive get intimately involved with the conversation or negotiation when he believes that a work action is right on the horizon. This allows the labor leaders and association members (employees) to know that he is "listening," and the issue is not something that is seen to be unimportant. With the executive becoming involved in the conversations and understanding the position of the labor unit firsthand, he may be able to provide a more efficient compromise or at least explain the position and reasoning of the institution/organization more appropriately than other administrators or individuals who are part of the compromise.

The school executive showing such an interest also enhances the respect he will garner from his employees, where now since he is attempting to work out the issues it becomes much more difficult for them to set forth a work action—or at least—a competent action. A work action will "wither away" when employees feel that their needs are being addressed by the executive. Hence, while the school executive is physically involved in the day-to-day discussions, work actions are unlikely to occur.

**Keep the lines of communication open.**

A major strategy utilized in thwarting any type of action is keeping the lines of communication with the labor unit open and transparent. It must be well known by the school executive and the leadership team that there is willingness on the management side to continue to compromise and address the concerns brought to them by the employees. Should the communication become stagnant or seem nonexistent, the intensity of the need for action will grow, and the executive may be faced with the need to make decisions and start over in consideration of negotiating terms or meeting the needs of her workforce.

Instead, through a transparent and open communication system, the school executive must make it known that communication is in a healthy place, even though both sides haven't made any concessions. As long as the means and process are still intact and fluid, communication should prevent any further discussions surrounding intensifying work actions and a drop in worker morale.

**Don't point too many "fingers" or place blame on who or what brought upon this impasse in the first place.**

Okay. So, everyone knows it's not the school executive's fault that this impasse is occurring (Hmm?). Regardless, the process will not move forward when and if the leadership keeps pointing fingers at members on the labor side. This includes not only association leaders, but all of the workers in the trenches who are the real reason why the organization reports the way it does.

Now, don't read this the wrong way. This coaching point doesn't reflect any school executive standing by and taking the blame for the impasse while being berated by employees and labor leaders who are in opposition. That is something that the executive must work to handle in a more immediate fashion through the utilization of her knowledge in leading the organization.

Rather, there is no benefit of blaming the "other" side. In fact, by placing blame on the employees or their representation, the school executive most likely will be seen as a "bully" or as an individual who is using a factor of intimidation to create an advantage. Usually, coming across as the "fairer" individual goes farther in consideration of earning a greater trust of the members in the organization.

**Know your BATNA. Remember the key points of negotiating and understand that to find a compromise is to also win.**

Students of the art of negotiation prepare for compromise by identifying the best alternative to the negotiated agreement (BATNA). The school executive can avoid any confrontation and work action while gaining the greater respect from her teams by growing morale if she knows where her potential to compromise on terms begins and ends. Therefore, the ability of an executive to truly know where she will be comfortable with said compromise is important prior to entering any discussions with labor leadership and other employee wants.

Firmly acknowledging what compromise the school executive feels would serve as a benefit to the organization allows him to arm his playbook with an incredible power of influence as a decision that fits within the scope of the BATNA could make him look more like a hero than the ultimate "boss villain." Let's look at an example.

A school district's employees are looking for compensation with regard to an extra technical application they needed to include in their lesson planning that falls within the scope of the contract parameters but took an extensive amount of time to produce. The outcome for the executive led to greater scores than was first realized, and it is in the executive's best interest to keep morale high so that production continues to grow in consideration of this new application.

The school executive heard rumblings of diminished morale and was aware that certain leaders were looking to approach him for additional compensation or construct a slowdown of work production until some demands were met. The executive agreed to a meeting, but first he "scrubbed" the data and formulated a BATNA that would continue to advance production and still elevate morale. The BATNA was a number in which the school executive and board could be comfortable with while still generating enough increased scoring margins in representation of the district's standards.

A meeting took place, and the employees sent a representative group who laid out several demands and a compensation schedule that they had worked on and believed was fair for both sides (administration and labor). Consequently, the amount for compensation that was requested was still lower than that of the BATNA that the executive had already thought could be a possibility. This now left the educational leader in a great position to facilitate a change in contract provision while still maintaining high returns, enhancing morale, and garnering respect from his employees.

**Meet more often than less often when trying to avoid or end a work action.**

When a work/job action is imminent or already in effect, it is important for the school executive to meet more often than less often so as to ensure that the labor side sees a willingness to come to an agreement quickly. Even just the perception of his working to come to some type of agreement will diminish the strength of the opposing campaign, and it will usually sever any support that employees have for the original reasoning behind the action in the first place.

## COACHES CORNER

Work actions that take place at schools and universities always paint a poor image of the administrator, executive, or board that is "causing" the action to occur. In the majority of cases, perception takes over and most of the information shared with the community and stakeholders comes from the labor and union side. This happens because management is bound by confidentiality issues where a release of information may lead to an unfair practice.

The perception that management is always to blame comes through when an action occurs. The solidarity of the labor force or union to stand behind such an important issue causes the layperson to take notice of the conflict, which may lead parents and other community members to become involved in a situation with which they have no true reason to be involved. The argument will always be that certain constituent groups do have some "stake" in the game, but the true reality is that the only way to become fully involved in a disagreement and potential compromise is to know both sides.

## YOU MAKE THE CALL: CASE SCENARIO

The scenario in chapter 19 included an action that occurred where union laborers were not employed by a professional services provider (construction manager) used by your organization.

> What plays would you call to avoid any such action from occurring in the future?
>
> Consider setting up some parameters with your labor leaders to communicate the importance of such concerns prior to them taking place. How would you handle that type of situation?

*Chapter 23*

# To Be or Not to Be

## *When Something Is or Isn't the Appropriate Decision*

Compromise can be seen as a weakness if it is done out of a fear for retribution. The school executive may take part in certain actions that are seen as harmful or egregious in nature, but they may be necessary to the overall importance of the mission, interactions, political atmosphere, or overall needs of the organization.

A strong leader who concentrates on fostering firm relationships with her employees and teams examines the types of differences between labor and management and what truly can or cannot be included when attempting to negotiate terms or come to a compromise.

First, it is absolutely imperative that every executive leader respects a strict code of ethics and examines each decision thoroughly. Then, each consideration is thoroughly reviewed through a lens that defines the moral, ethical, and legal ramifications of every decision.

### MORAL, ETHICAL, AND LEGAL CONSIDERATIONS (MEL): THE EXECUTIVE'S LITMUS TEST[1]

Every decision that a chief executive in a company or organization makes must first include a litany of considerations with regard to how said decision will directly affect the personnel, stakeholder groups, and company/organization as a whole. With each decision made, the executive must weigh the moral, ethical, and legal considerations that may stem from the directive from the executive.

With each of these considerations, the school executive must also review her playbook to understand the tactics and protocols that can be utilized when determining what actions are appropriate when compromising and directing employees to complete tasks, interact with the public and entities from other businesses or groups, and make decisions that are in the best interest of the organization and the school executive herself. Decisions can also include the encouragement of actions from others that may lead to an unfavorable outcome or make others "uncomfortable."

This doesn't mean that those directives or decisions include plays that are designed to hurt or purposely disrupt the progression of positive experiences for the individuals at hand and the organization outright.

Regardless, it is the school executive's duty—yes, his absolute duty—to consider MEL prior to making every decision that deals with his professional experiences as they relate to other individuals who fall within his purview of supervision and leadership oversight. After each of those considerations are made and the value of their perceived outcomes are analyzed by the executive himself, he can rest assured that the decisions made and directives given, no matter how popular or unpopular they may seem to be to others around him, have been vetted for appropriateness and with the intent to shield those under his charge from any harm or wrongdoing.

## (M)ORAL CONSIDERATIONS

With each decision that the school executive makes that includes a charge to her employees, supervisors, or labor workforce, she must look to any moral implications that may arise from that decision or directive. Moral decision making includes an ability of the leader/executive to choose the correct course of action based on appropriate standards of behavior and beliefs when determining what is the "right" and "wrong" thing to do. A moral consideration is based on a standard that supports a behavior that would allow individuals within the group to work and "live" in cooperation with one another.

One of the biggest concerns when reviewing the moral consideration of decisions that the school executive may make includes the notion that everyone has different morals and values. Morality is shaped by an individual's personal upbringing, political views, and other factors that we inherit from our development as children on our journey through adolescence. Moral values can be defined as an individual's intent to show honesty; following certain principles; being kind and considerate to others; and following through on a purposeful course of action to make a difference in the lives of others.

The school executive must consider all of these factors when assuring that his decisions with regard to his employees, labor leaders, and other areas of compromise meet a high moral standard. This standard includes a strong professional and personal character while defining what the "right thing" is to do that will affect the most people throughout the organization.

## (E)THICAL CONSIDERATIONS

Most every company, business, or organization will have a code of ethics that was designed in conjunction with a stakeholder group and outlines the values, morals, and missions of the entity as a whole. Also, industries, fields of study, educational institutions, and governmental elected offices all have ethical foundations and codes that must be followed to remain in good standing. Something that maintains a level of appropriate ethics stays within the parameters set forth by the code or association.

The school executive's decisions must be considered ethical in order to remain in good standing and considered fair and reasonable. To go outside the parameters set forth by the ethical code would be to breach the established code and create a situation that is not morally correct in the eyes of the institution.

## (L)EGAL CONSIDERATIONS

There are many laws and statutes that govern and oversee the legal limitations of institutions and the decisions that school executives will make that affect the working conditions and negotiated actions of the workforce in an organization. The preceding chapters in the text include some of the legal standards, case law, and acts that outline the leader-labor relationship and what can or cannot be done when making decisions based on interactions between the school executive and her teams of employees and other stakeholder groups.

Some of the major issues and laws surrounding labor and the workforce involve discrimination and harassment; leaves due to family illness and maternity; wrongful termination; disputes about wages and hours; misclassification of job status and prescribed duties; unsafe working conditions; and worker's compensation for on-the-job injuries.

In determining which directive to give or "plays" to use in an individual situation with an employee or in dealing with union labor leadership, it is imperative that the school executive understands that she is not "breaking" any labor laws or deciding to include actions that may be seen as arbitrary and capricious.[2] On their own, some directives may seem to be egregious and detrimental to workers and be viewed as though the workers' conditions are not being considered or respected with regard to the needs of both the institution and each individual. However, the executive must take a deeper dive and be sure that what she is demanding of her team is the product of true compromise and an established high legal standard.

Overall, it is the ultimate responsibility of the school executive to make the right decision when choosing to direct an employee or interpreting an employee's contract. Whether it is a decision that is made directly to the worker from the executive, discussing a collectively bargained agreement with union leadership, or a liaison/representative acting on behalf of a union or group of employees, the school executive must know whether her decision is or is not appropriate in consideration of the moral, ethical, and legal litmus test that should be completed before each and every decision is made.

Therefore, regardless of what the actual decision is, at minimum she understands the ramifications and possible fallout that may be received based on the directive that she gives to her team of employees.

## COACHES CORNER

There will come a time (or two) when an educational leader will make the wrong decision. The main consideration when evaluating such outcomes includes whether or not the executive used as much relevant information and data as possible and if the executive made concessions based on what she thought would be best for her students and employees.

At times, decisions must be made because the climate of the community or the nation dictates changes be made based on an action or a response to some type of movement based on an event or lack of a response to that event. Educational systems have always been a beacon for individuals, movements, and causes due to the simple fact that each educational system represents a true microcosm of our society.

Each and every education network across the nation includes a stratified socioeconomic contingent, representatives from all political groups, and individuals who are both pro and con in consideration of social issues and local differences that affect the economy, family values, and the state of the nation as a whole.

Therefore, certain decisions and attempts to compromise must be made that will challenge families and students to make difficult concessions or follow specific procedures and protocols that they may otherwise not support. The same holds true for the day-to-day impact that the decisions of the executive have on his constituents and labor force.

In all, not every decision will be supported and applauded by every member of the district or institution. Simply put, the executive cannot make everyone happy all of the time. However, as long as the best interests of the system are aligned with what leads to the ultimate decision that is made, the executive can leave each decision knowing that he did all he can to help effectuate a change that would benefit some portion of the constituents who he serves.

## YOU MAKE THE CALL: CASE SCENARIO

Niccolo Ford has been your director of information technology for the last six years. After several meetings with his team, it had been decided that a consulting firm must be hired in order to assist employees in finding appropriate vendors and consolidate transportation routes in order to accommodate greater pupil transport within specific budget parameters. When it reaches your office as chief education officer, you agree with the findings.

Several consulting firms apply to the request for proposals that was posted online and in the local newspaper, and the board trustees are set to discuss the final candidates with you and approve the consultant at an upcoming board meeting.

It has come to your attention through several of your employees and their labor liaison that no interviews had taken place, and the consultant that was being recommended for hire was a company named SCS, whose lead consultant is Mr. Ford's son-in-law.

Although this consultant may be the best suited for the position, the perception of the selection process by your workforce and the lack of transparency from Mr. Ford to your office with regard to the selection of the firm is somewhat troubling.

> How do you handle the situation?
> What plays do you call?
> What are your moral, ethical, and legal considerations for hiring a firm or vendor?
> What should have been Mr. Ford's moral, ethical, and legal considerations at the onset of this scenario?

## NOTES

1. A test used to see if something is effective and decisive.
2. A decision made without reasonable grounds or adequate consideration of the circumstances.

*Chapter 24*

# The Goldilocks Approach

*Not Too Hot, and Not Too Cold*

We all remember the fairy tale we heard as young children, *Goldilocks and the Three Bears*. The "Goldilocks Principle" assumes that individuals experience a heightened level of motivation when they work on projects and directives that push them to use a skill set and knowledge base that measures up to their capabilities. Nothing too hard, and nothing too easy.

The school executive has her playbook filled with plays to be utilized to help her influence her team to meet the goals she has established to remain successful in an ever-changing world. One of her most important attributes in leading such a diverse and hardworking labor force must be her ability to know the capabilities of each employee on her team and be able to lead them past their limitations.

She does this by ensuring their tasks and job descriptions are not too hard—and not too easy. She follows up with an approach that's not too hot—and not too cold. Keeping this in mind, the school executive provides the perfect formula for strengthening labor relations and effectively navigating the workplace, politics, and conflicts with personnel and union leadership.

She continues to add to her playbook, referencing those leadership skills, tactics, and maneuvers that she finds are successful when addressing her employees and any of their representatives. It's apparent to her that she needs to ensure that her workforce feels respected, appreciated, and wholly understands that not one person in the organization is any more important than the next person.

Although she keeps the playbook close and references it often, she knows too well the twenty plays by heart that are essential to ensuring the success of the organization and each individual himself. By utilizing and practicing these plays over, and over, and over, she creates a climate and culture in the workplace that will boost morale and elevate levels of production by increasing an independent work ethic that will spread exponentially to all members in the organization.

Keeping grounded and living by the not too hot . . . not too cold mentality, the school executive understands that she must utilize these plays to the best of her ability, and she needs to attempt to meet the needs of all of her workforce either individually or by group as often as possible. If working with a labor association or union leadership, she understands that working with them is the same as working with all of her employees, and compromise is a form of communication that will give her the greatest advantage over any adversity she may encounter on her leadership journey.

These plays are designed to cause the executive to lead by example; to place the onus on herself and on her role rather than blaming anyone else in the organization for any mishap, bad rating, or wrongdoing; to remind the executive to always live the "team" mentality; and to understand that admitting when one is wrong is right.

## THE SCHOOL EXECUTIVE'S PLAYBOOK: TOP TWENTY PLAYS[1]

### #1: Don't sweat the small stuff.

There are too many moving parts in an institution or organization on a daily basis to get too involved in the things that are too time-consuming to handle. In other words, don't micromanage.

Often, leaders and school executives get caught in the trap of involving themselves in the minutiae of planning and become unable to remain focused on other things or the overall issue at hand. The school executive that refuses to let the "small stuff" control his day and work schedule will be able to extend the involvement of his workforce and provide some autonomy to think creatively and work more freely.

### #2: Be the coach!

Good players cannot run plays effectively without coaxing from their coach. Members of the labor force or association leadership need to take direction from the school executive to be able to concentrate on other, more productive things. Coaches guide, encourage, cry and laugh with, and support their team members by providing the wisdom, insight, and tools to get the job done.

### #3: Say "hello" and get to know who they are.

No one wants to "run through a wall" for the school executive or leader who won't pick his head up to say, "hello" or offer a smile. The school executive who refuses to make cordial greetings should stay in his office and start packing up his stuff! This type of negativity is absolutely contagious from top down, and it will greatly affect production and morale in a negative manner.

Further, getting to know the names and interests of the labor team will help the school executive fit in and truly be considered as part of the team. No one needs to go making "best friends"; however, showing an interest and staying in tune with the staff goes a very long way.

### #4: Have their backs.

Another big play for the school executive is to always support her team in consideration of external influences or conditions that are beyond the scope of her control. An employee or member of the workforce who feels the support from his executive when times are bad, as well as when they are good, will provide a greater sense of respect and loyalty towards the executive.

### #5: Be consistent.

Nothing is worse for creating a recipe for success than an individual's inability to be consistent. This especially holds true for the school executive who gives one worker one thing and another worker with the same conditions something else.

This is always a concern for the school district or higher education institution, understanding that it is difficult to maintain consistency in all of the systems in the organization with the numerous different leadership styles of supervisors, administrators, and managers. Inconsistency among these managers may lead to problems at the office, internal struggles, advancing politics, and other concerns for the school executive's edification purposes.

### #6: Make people feel safe.

Any student of Maslow[2] first believed that the goal of the hierarchy of needs was to reach the apex and make as much compensation and fringe benefits as possible. On the contrary, the "needs pyramid" would only crumble if concentration was not placed on the foundation of the structure. It is absolutely necessary that an employee's physiological needs must be secure in order for their motivation to feel heightened and their productivity increase.

This physiological need includes water, food, sleep, and warmth. If you add in the work environment as well, job security provides for a strong foundation to build upon so an employee doesn't feel threatened with a loss of work or wages.

#7: **Don't preach.**

No one wants to be "talked to." An employee who is wrong and who is admonished for it—gets it. By preaching, the school executive may come across like she knows more than the rest of her team members and workers. This does not help build morale in the workplace.

#8: **Decrease workplace tension.**

The school executive must mediate any concern among employees and issues that arise to help decrease tensions in the workplace. When a union, labor association, or workplace liaison is involved in the organization, the leadership should assist the school executive in mediating any differences among employees.

#9: **Be "friendly" but not "friends."**

As a follow-up to the "smile" play, the school executive must adopt a friendly demeanor towards his labor unit, but be careful to not befriend them over social media or at bars, restaurants, etc. Sometimes, this can be a difficult transition for the executive and workers, especially if he "came up through the ranks" with them.

#10: **Make sure they have what they need to be successful.**

A house cannot be built without tools. The same holds true for the mental, social, psychological, and physical tools that the workforce needs to get the job accomplished. The school executive must "check-in" from time to time to see if his team members are getting what they need to be successful—in consideration of all areas of wellness and productivity.

## #11: Spotlight what employees are capable of doing successfully.

Individuals want to feel important, and the school executive who shares the employees' successes and accomplishments with others goes a long way with the entire organization. In fact, shining the proverbial spotlight on individuals who have gone above and beyond the executive's expectations is nothing less than contagious. By spotlighting employees and other members of her team, the school executive will in effect be shining a spotlight on the positive influences she has made over her organization as well.

## #12: Empower them to go beyond their potential.

The school executive can use this play to provide time, incentives, program development, and lateral job promotions with title changes for employees in the workforce who go beyond their potential to try new initiatives and expand the footprint of the organization. The key here is that the executive must first "empower" her teams by finding ways to offer this beyond the regular work schedule.

## #13: Remember where you came from.

Most often, the school executive wasn't born an executive, and he climbed the proverbial ladder to reach this point in his career development in the education field or a related industry. It is an extremely important play in the playbook for the school executive to revisit his roots often when the occasion arises.

As the school executive looks around the office or classroom, he sees himself many years before making some of the same decisions and mistakes that these individuals and veteran employees make on a daily basis. The executive needs to step back and take notice of the days, years, and decades that it took him to develop professionally and create the resume he currently has in his possession.

## #14: Buy lunch from time to time.

A great play for the school executive is to come into the office and order a few pizzas for everyone for lunch. Or how about some sandwiches? Once, I grabbed my team and we left at noon and watched a movie together at the local Cineplex. I also recall working near New York City, and my direct supervisor used to drive me through the Lincoln Tunnel and I would jump out of the car, buy a few bags of roasted cashews, and we would head back to school with a bag for the principal (and of course, his secretary). These aren't actions to waste time, but rather they are events used to help build relationships with the most important members in your work world.

#15: Put employees in a position of influence and leadership.

Great school executives provide opportunities for the workforce and labor unit members to facilitate programs, meetings, etc. and influence effective leadership throughout the ranks in an organization. There are many employees and team members who do not want the role of an administrator, department coach, or supervisor because of the stress and responsibilities that are attached to it; however, they may appreciate an opportunity to expand their role in the organization by helping to effectuate change while facilitating a service to the work community in a different capacity.

#16: Share your success and make it their success.

It's quite all right for the school executive to share how he rates his success within the organization. However, it is extremely important that those statements also include a decree that the executive is "only successful when his entire team is successful," or his "success stems only from their successes."

#17: Encourage them to advance their own personal development.

The school executive leader who provides a road map for professional development for her staff is fulfilling part of her own job description and goals by leading her personnel to develop professionally in consideration of improvements that may be needed. By encouraging the unit to advance professionally on their own accord, the school executive allows time for the individual employee to reflect on his own needs and wants, and prompts him to move forward on his own in search of an enhancement in a skill and knowledge that will benefit him, his colleagues, and all stakeholder groups.

#18: Compel employees to work together.

When establishing groups of employees to support one another on a mission for the organization, it is an important part of the play that the school executive attempts to group individuals who haven't been together prior to that afternoon. This will not only allow individuals to learn from one another, but it will also allow individuals to strengthen their own relationships with different employees and provide insight for employees as to the strengths and weaknesses of other members of the organization.

### #19: Provide feedback loops.

Feedback and evaluation are extremely important, but providing feedback loops will allow the school executive to understand programmatic, personnel, and company issues while directing protocols to include an open-ended sequence to ensure an advanced dialogue between leadership and labor exists more often than not.

### #20: Be human.

This one is simple—you either have this play or you don't.

## COACHES CORNER

Educational leaders and school executives must be sure to handle each and every situation they deal with as an individual situation. Educational executives are taught early on in their leadership careers that being consistent is the only way to be successful and gain the most respect from all members of the district, school, or institution. Just like we develop teachers to perform classroom management strategies in a consistent fashion so as not to create any student outliers, educational leaders must also use a consistent approach when handling matters that deal with their labor workforce, teachers, and support staff.

The impression that the executive makes on her faculty and staff depends on how often she uses her tone and actions to support or admonish individuals and her teams for specific actions that are a cause for concern within the system.

The school executive who rules by fear, "yells," and argues with her team members about their actions will cause her power to be attenuated based on her demeanor and focus on micromanaging other leaders while sharing that she does not have faith in their potential to run their part of the organization effectively. This comes across as "too hot," and it is difficult for any executive to recuperate from these types of reactions to conflict and decision-making inferences.

On the other hand, the executive must, at the most appropriate times, wield her power and prove to her team that she is not taking a muted or restrained approach to a situation that has come to the forefront. Although this doesn't have to be an extremely "forceful" response, it must be indicative of the executive needing an assurance that what has occurred will be corrected or handled in an appropriate manner.

It also must be made clear through her reaction that the school executive is always aware of the happenings around the district, school, or academic institution, even though she may not physically be there all of the time. The bottom line is that there must be some response to an intervention or an action that was taken in consideration of an issue at hand or something that has come to the executive's desk.

Every decision that the school executive makes must be handled . . . well, just right! One can concede that when navigating the workplace, politics, and the conflicts that arise with personnel and union leadership, finding the perfect formula takes time when dealing with different needs and personalities. This includes those needs, values, and expectations of the educational leader herself. It is important that each situation and decision be made knowing how specific words and actions will dictate the outcome based on the individuals involved.

## YOU MAKE THE CALL: CASE SCENARIO

Your institution labor representative, Connie Loper, wants to speak with you about several concerns that she has regarding working conditions at your North End campus. You meet with Connie, and she begins by telling you about a situation she has at home with one of her daughters who is looking for a job during the summer break from college.

As she moves into the issue, she begins to explain that one of your receptionists, Angelica Grieco, is having a difficult time at home with one of her children who is having an issue in school and was just suspended. She has had to leave early on several occasions, and several other workers had to "pick up the slack" to keep the production in the office up to the level of your expectations.

No one has complained up to this point—it has been several weeks, and the team has been making it work. Now, some of the other administrative assistants are looking for extra compensation for their time and more support in the office.

There are state reports and evaluations that are due soon, and the supervisors are getting nervous.

What plays do you call?
What are some of the pros and cons of the situation that is occurring?
What are your next steps?

## NOTES

1. Adapted in part from Glenn Lopis, "6 Things Wise Leaders Do To Engage Their Employees," *Forbes*, February 2, 2015.

2. Maslow's hierarchy of needs outlines that motivation is the result of a person's attempt at fulfilling five basic needs (physiological, safety, social, esteem, and self-actualization).

*Chapter 25*

# Impact of Important Labor Court Cases, Legal Considerations, and Precedents[1]

Throughout history, federal, state, and local courts have decided disputes between citizens, businesses, and organizations, and have formed decisions that set precedents that help to resolve future disputes around the United States. The same holds true for incidents involving the management-labor relationship and the rights of employees to form unions.

Attorneys, resource directors, boards, and chief executives utilize case law to provide an evidentiary knowledge base for recommendations and decisions; creating policies and parameters for programs; and negotiating contracts and other amendments to working conditions, compensation, and time.

Important decisions from courts have helped to shape the landscape of the management-labor relationship since the early twentieth century. In fact, one can argue that the cases and decisions are reflective of the needs of the workforce relative to conditions surrounding the country during that specific time and in consideration of societal and economic norms that establish the commitment of each generation to ensuring the delivery of inalienable rights to all citizens.

An example of this would include the changing technological needs of an advancing world where new industries are being created, and several industries that will be needed aren't even close to being established yet. We continue to be a society of progress and change that has witnessed children work in jobs some twenty years later that didn't exist when they were six years old.

Although these decisions and labor protections through organized unions are arguably the backbone and foundation for what helped to build the United States as to where it is today, many states have provided a legal basis for businesses and individuals to work free from union or labor association involvement in consideration of employment opportunities throughout industries.

Known as a "right-to-work" state, legislation enacted by lawmakers guarantees that no individual can be forced as a condition of his or her employment to join or pay dues or fees to a labor union.

A state has the right to enact these laws under the protection of the National Labor Relations Act (NLRA), Section 14(b). Figure 25.1 represents the states that are considered "right-to-work" states, but these regulations frequently change as the needs of each states' workers change and elections bring new legislators with their own agendas and the agendas of their own constituent base to the forefront.

Regardless of the choice of an individual to have representation or not, the case law and labor legislation help to establish parameters necessary for bargaining and other considerations that an executive needs to ensure that her workforce remains productive and competitive within her industry. The following lists several cases that have impacted specific areas of labor relationships over several different industries over the last century. The group includes Supreme and Appeals Court precedents, and federal cases as they apply to disputes in the workforce and compulsory unionism.

## 2020—*Bostock v. Clayton County*, 590 U.S.

Considered a landmark decision of the Supreme Court, *Bostock v. Clayton County* held that Title VII prohibits discrimination against employees based

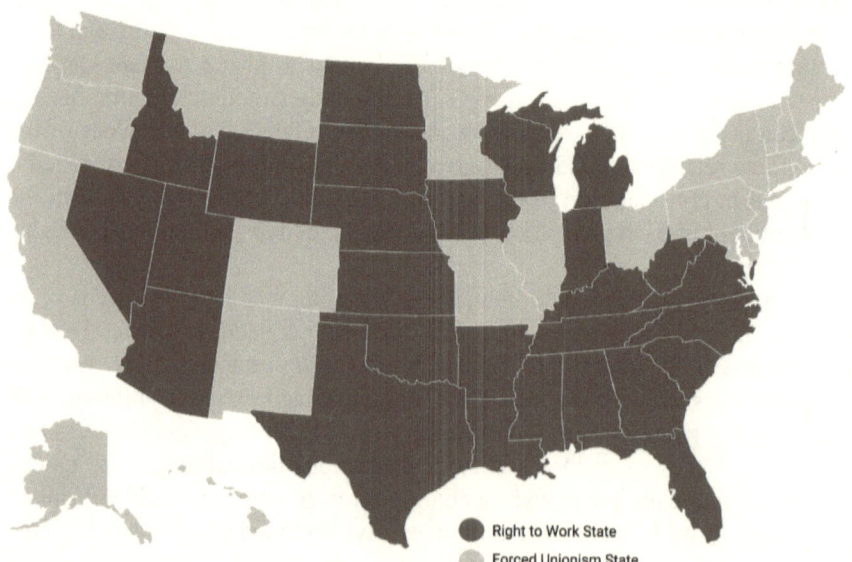

Figure 25.1. Right to Work States, 2021. National Right to Work Legal Defense Foundation.

upon their sexual orientation and their transgender status. The 6-3 decision with an opinion by Justice Gorsuch upheld that

> for an employer to discriminate against employees for being homosexual or transgender, the employer must intentionally discriminate against individual men and women in part because of sex. . . . That has always been prohibited by Title VII's plain terms—and that should be the end of the analysis.

### 2019—*Alex Morgan v. United States Soccer Federation*

Twenty-eight players from the U.S. Women's National Soccer Team filed a lawsuit against the United States Soccer Federation in 2019 citing violations under the Equal Pay Act and Title VII of the Civil Rights Act. The suit claimed pay disparities and "unequal playing conditions" in consideration of men and women who played on the same national teams.

Although a settlement was reached that addresses the differences, the equal pay claims in the lawsuit were dismissed in district court, citing that although the Equal Pay Act prohibits pay disparity based on sex, the team's collective-bargaining agreements created the disparity, therefore ruling out the issue of sex discrimination.

### 2018—*Janus v. AFSCME*

The Supreme Court held in a 5 to 4 decision that nonunion government workers cannot be required to pay union fees as a condition of working in public service. In other words, it is not permissible to "charge" fees or dues to nonunion individuals because they are working under a union contract.

The court overturned *Abood* (see below 1977) which agreed that fees could be imposed on public employees to the extent that they are used for collective-bargaining. Janus outlines that forcing public employees to pay any union fees is compelled speech and unconstitutional under the First Amendment.

### 2014—*Harris v. Quinn*

The Supreme Court held in a 5 to 4 decision that a requirement for non-union, Medicaid-funded home-care personal assistants in Illinois to pay fees to their union violates the First Amendment. The first refusal to extend *Abood* was affirmed "[b]ecause of Abood's questionable foundations, and because the personal assistants are quite different from full-fledged public employees."

## 2012—*Knox v. Service Employees International Union*

In an opinion by Justice Alito, the Supreme Court held 5-4 that "when a public sector union imposes a special assessment or dues increase, the union must provide [a notice of the purpose of the assessment or increase] and may not exact any funds from nonmembers without their affirmative consent." The decision also held that a union could not charge nonunion members for its expenses created in opposing ballot questions even if they affect future contracts or conditions.

## 2009—*Locke v. Karass*, 555 U.S. 207

The court's decision held that the First Amendment permits a local union to charge every nonmember public employee for the purpose of paying fees for national litigation expenses for other bargaining units if said litigation somehow relates to the collective-bargaining agreement and the charge is "reciprocal in nature."

## 2008—*Chamber of Commerce v. Brown*, 554 U.S. 60

Pursuant to the decision of the court, the National Labor Relations Act comes before a state statute that prohibits companies (that receive state grants or funding) from using funds to deter union organizing.

## 2007—*Davenport v. Washington Education Association*

In a unanimous decision, the court found that where unions have no constitutional right to collect fees from nonmembers, a state can require that a union obtains affirmative consent before spending any nonmember public employee forced fees on decided political activities of the association.

## 1998—*Marquez v. Screen Actors Guild (SAG)*

With its decision, the court held that a union does not breach its duty of fair representation through its negotiation of a "compulsory unionism" provision that claims workers must be union members in good standing in order to maintain employment. The court also declared that, if a union negotiates a compulsory unionism provision, it must notify workers that they can satisfy the requirement by paying fees to support the union's collective bargaining and contract without becoming active members.

## 1998—*Air Line Pilots Association v. Miller*

Supreme Court Justice Ginsburg delivered the opinion in a 7-2 ruling that states employees, who did not agree to union arbitration procedures, cannot be compelled to utilize the arbitration process before challenging the amount of their fees for collective bargaining in a federal court action.

## 1996—*Brown v. Pro Football,* 518 U.S. 231, 116 S. Ct. 2116

The court affirmed the finding of the appellate court, which held that members of the NFL did not violate the Sherman Act through their implementation of unilateral changes to the contract after reaching impasse. The court agreed that a non-statutory labor exemption shields from federal antitrust laws since the owners made a "good-faith wage offer" to team members who would be placed on a developmental squad program, there was no basis for distinguishing football players from other organized workers (e.g., developmental squad), and the non-statutory labor exemption applied to the NFL's unilateral implementation of the developmental squad program.

## 1995—*NLRB v. Town & Country Elec.,* 516 U.S. 85, 116 S. Ct. 450

The U.S. Court of Appeals for the 8th Circuit expressed the opinion after an arbitration that people working for a particular company while also being paid by a union to organize that company were not considered company employees under the National Labor Relations Act and not protected from anti-union discrimination.

The Supreme Court then decided the meaning of the word "employee" as it upheld that a worker may be an "employee" of said company (pursuant to the tenets of the National Labor Relations Act) even if the union compensates that same worker to help organize the company for the union. The court agreed that the board's decision was lawful because the term "employee" was defined with a broad language consistent with the Act and common law. Service to the union for pay did not involve abandonment of work duties to the company because the union organizers could limit their organizing duties to nonworking hours.

## 1991—*Lehnert v. Ferris Faculty Association*

In *Lehnert,* the court concluded that union activities are not chargeable to objecting nonmembers unless they are (1) "germane to collective-bargaining activity" and (2) "do not significantly add to the burdening of free speech that is inherent in allowance of an agency or union shop."

## 1989—*Ohio Public Employees Retirement System v. Betts,* 492 U.S. 158

The Supreme Court held that the Age Discrimination Employment Act does not prohibit discrimination in an employee's benefit plan unless said plan discriminates in consideration of a "non-fringe" benefit of the individual worker's employment. Betts had originally claimed that her benefits plan discriminated against her on the basis of age.

## 1988—*Communications Workers of America v. Beck*

The court held that only fees and dues necessary to perform the duties of an exclusive representative of the employees in dealing with labor-management issues were permissible. Thus, private sector employees have the same right not to subsidize union non-bargaining activities as railway, airline, and other public entities.

## 1986—*Meritor Savings Bank v. Vinson*

In *Vinson*, the Supreme Court ruled that sexual harassment in the workplace leading to a hostile environment was considered gender discrimination and a violation of Title VII of the Civil Rights Act. Before this case appeared in front of the high court, sexual harassment could only be tied to a discrimination claim if the harassment resulted in some type of quantifiable material loss by the employee (e.g., lost wages, termination). The facts before the Supreme Court had provided that Title VII was not exclusive to covering only discrimination on the basis of gender that led only to material losses.

## 1986—*Chicago Teachers Union v. Hudson*

In a unanimous decision, the court held that First Amendment due process requires procedural safeguards must be established before compulsory union fees can be collected from public employees. This includes notice of the basis for a fee, reasonably impartial review of nonmembers' challenges, and escrow of "amounts reasonably in dispute" while challenges are pending.

## 1985—*Pattern Makers v. National Labor Relations Board*

The Supreme Court upheld that private sector workers had the right to resign their union membership immediately.

### 1983—*Knight v. Minnesota Community College Faculty Association*, 460 U.S. 1048

The court affirmed a lower court's decision that rejected the argument that exclusive representation of public employees by a union is unconstitutional because it can force an association with a political action organization.

### 1979—*Smith v. Arkansas State Highway Employees*, 441 U.S. 463 (per curiam)

The court held (per curiam) that the First Amendment does not provide an obligation on the part of government . . . to recognize any type of labor organization or union and collectively bargain with said union.

### 1977—*Abood v. Detroit Board of Education*

The court rejected the argument made that requiring public employees to pay agency fees to keep their jobs violates the First Amendment. In *Abood*, the court ruled the fees constitutionally valid "insofar as the service charges are applied to collective bargaining, contract administration, and grievance-adjustment purposes."

The court did unanimously agree that "a union cannot constitutionally spend [objectors'] funds for the expression of political views, on behalf of political candidates, or toward the advancement of other ideological causes not germane to its duties as collective-bargaining representative." This established grounds for changes to be made decades later, and mentioned in the aforementioned cases (Janus, Harris).

### 1976—*City of Charlotte v. Firefighters Local 660*, 426 U.S. 283

The court upheld that a public employer is not obligated to provide payroll deductions for union dues.

### 1976—*Oil Workers v. Mobil Oil Corp.*, 426 U.S. 407

The court held that the "situs" of an employee determines whether a state's Right to Work law applies to the condition. In this case, seamen are not protected by the Right to Work law of the state in which they were hired.

## 1976—City of Madison Joint School District No. 8 v. Wisconsin Employment Relations Commission, 429 U.S. 167

The court ruled that a state may not require school boards to prohibit nonunion teachers from speaking against collective agreements at public meetings.

## 1974—Geduldig v. Aiello, 417 U.S. 484 (plus General Electric Co. v. Gilbert [1976])

The Supreme Court found that the classification of normal pregnancy as non-compensable was not a "sex-based" classification and the denial of insurance benefits for work loss resulting from pregnancy did not violate the 14th Amendment. Although the court was clear that the denial had to be rationalized by the state, the Supreme Court extended their reasoning to include Title VII in *General Electric Co. v. Gilbert*, in 1976. Then, in 1978, Congress usurped the *Gilbert* ruling with the passage of the Pregnancy Discrimination Act of 1978, amending Title VII and making it clear that pregnancy discrimination constitutes sex discrimination.

## 1971—Griggs v. Duke Power Co.

The Supreme Court held that the tenets of the Civil Rights Act prohibited employers from barring employees from certain positions based on level of education or aptitude of tests when said position did not require the candidate to pass a proficiency exam or expertise in the area.

## 1963—Railway Clerks v. Allen, 373 U.S. 113

The court held that nonunion members, who notify union leadership of their desire for proof of the proportion of union expenses, are entitled to said records since unions maintain all pertinent facts and records in consideration of operations.

## 1963—National Labor Relations Board v. General Motors, 373 U.S. 734

The court upheld that the "union shop" may require payment of initiation fees and dues as a condition of employment, but may not require formal membership.

## 1954—*Radio Officers' Union v. National Labor Relations Board,* 347 U.S. 17

The court ruled that compulsory unionism agreements may not be used "for any purpose other than to compel payment of union dues and fees." Thus, employees do not have to follow union rules or be considered "formal members" to maintain their employment status.

## 1949—*Lincoln Federal Labor Union v. Northwestern Iron & Metal Co.,* 335 U.S. 525

Here, the court ruled that state Right to Work laws are considered constitutional.

## 1949—*Algoma Plywood Co. v. Wisconsin Bd.,* 336 U.S. 301

The court agreed that the National Labor Relations Act (NLRA) permitted state Right to Work laws prior to the passage of Taft-Hartley Act amendments by Congress in 1947.

## 1944—*J. I. Case Co. v. National Labor Relations Board,* 321 U.S. 332 and *Order of Railroad Telegraphers v. Railway Express Agency, Inc.,* 321 U.S. 342

Although the question of constitutionality was not raised, the court interpreted that the National Labor Relations and Railway Labor Acts were prohibiting employees from negotiating their own terms and conditions for employment where a representative from a formal bargaining unit has been formally recognized.

## 1937—*Virginian Railway v. System Federation No. 40,* 300 U.S. 515 and *NLRB v. Jones & Laughlin Steel Corp.,* 301 U.S. 1

The court held that compulsory collective bargaining was constitutional; however, the constitutionality of bargaining units was not addressed since the complaints were brought forth by employers and not employees.

### COACHES CORNER

It is imperative that educational leaders utilize case precedent, state labor laws, and past practice as an evidentiary knowledge base when making decisions with regard to handling personnel in schools, districts, and institutions. Knowing what precedents have been established and the details surrounding those situations will give the executive the ability to establish a strong foundation for the reasoning behind the actions he took in response to a personnel action or a policy change he has implemented for the system at large.

Overall, not knowing what legal basis already exists for a situation prior to taking the action itself just isn't "smart" leadership. Most specifically in an education setting, being prepared shows strong leadership and will give the executive the advantage if she already knows what cases, situations, policies, and precedents may support a decision or educational choice she is about to make prior to disturbing the school district or educational institution.

## YOU MAKE THE CALL: CASE SCENARIO

Several of your teachers have approached you stating that they did not agree with some of the decisions made by their local union president. To them, it seems like the president doesn't respect the needs of all of the employees, and she just caters to the needs of those association members who are her closest friends.

The teachers want to remove themselves from their association with the local union.

> What plays do you call?
> What are the implications of employees meeting with you to leave their labor union and then leaving the union?
> What laws outline the protocols for such an interest?
> How much should a school executive get involved with such a request?
> When do you inform your attorney about the conversation?
> Do you inform the union leadership of your conversation with and the concerns of the teachers who approached you?

## NOTE

1. Section and case law adapted from: David I. Brody, "The Top 7 Recent Employment Law Cases You Should Know," Workforce, July 31, 2020; LexisNexis (various); the National Right to Work Legal Defense and Education Foundation Inc., Springfield, VA; National Institute for Labor Relations Research. (2021)

# About the Author

**Dr. Richard D. Tomko** has had numerous administrative responsibilities during his twenty-one-year career in educational administration. He has been a building administrator at the middle and secondary levels and responsible for district-wide curriculum, assessment, innovative program initiatives, technology, and professional development while in central office positions. Dr. Tomko has dedicated his career to serving communities as an educational leader, acting as a director, assistant principal, principal, assistant superintendent, and superintendent in both private and public school systems. He earned a doctor of philosophy degree in educational leadership, management, and policy from Seton Hall University; a master of jurisprudence from Loyola University Chicago School of Law; and holds certificates in community and economic development from Pennsylvania State University and the Brain, Mind, and Teaching certificate from Johns Hopkins University. He is an adjunct professor at Manhattan College, teaching in both the school building leadership and counseling programs; he also works as a consultant to educational institutions and families.

Dr. Tomko and his wife, Jaimie, cofounded WISPER (We Invest in Strong Programs, Empowerment, and building Respect for Women) a 501(c)3 established to assist and recognize individuals and their mentors who deserve support in helping to fulfill the mission of "Paying it Forward" by leveling the proverbial playing field in the spirit of equality for all through the advancement of leadership; nurturing of future career paths; representing community ideals; and enhancing academic standards in education.

Dr. Tomko is a change agent for creativity and problem-solving and works with administrative teams to decrease achievement gaps between demographic subgroups of learners by involving families, stakeholders, and community groups in the restoration of student engagement leading to overall student success.

www.ingramcontent.com/pod-product-compliance
Lightning Source LLC
Chambersburg PA
CBHW030141240426
43672CB00005B/214